Mighty Mikko

MIGHTY MIKKO

BY PARKER FILLMORE
CZECHOSLOVAK FAIRY TALES
THE SHOEMAKER'S APRON
Both Illustrated by Jan Matulka

THE LAUGHING PRINCE
Illustrated by Jay Van Everen

THE HICKORY LIMB
Illustrated by Rose Cecil O'Neill

THE ROSIE WORLD
Illustrated by Maginal Wright Enright

A Book of Finnish Fairy Tales and Folk Tales

BY
PARKER FILLMORE

WITH ILLUSTRATIONS AND DECORATIONS
BY
JAY VAN EVEREN

NEW YORK
HARCOURT, BRACE AND COMPANY

415
C78

A 580197

Copyright, 1922, by
PARKER FILLMORE

PRINTED IN THE U. S. A. BY
THE QUINN & BODEN COMPANY
RAHWAY, N J

To my niece

PHYLLIS

These stories of her mother's native land

NOTE

The spirit of nationalism that swept over the small peoples of Europe in the early nineteenth century touched faraway Finland and started the Finns on the quest of the Finnish. There as elsewhere scholars who were also patriots found that the native tongue, lost to the educated and the well-to-do, had been preserved in the songs and stories which were current among the peasants. Elias Lönnrot spent a long and busy life collecting those ancient *runos* from which he succeeded in building up a national epic, the *Kalevala*. This is Lönnrot's great contribution to his own country and to the world. Beside the material for the *Kalevala* Lönnrot made important collections of lyrics, proverbs, and stories.

During his time and since other patriot scholars have

made faithful records of the songs and tales which the old Finnish minstrels, the *runolaulajat,* chanted to the strains of the *kantele.* The mass of such material now gathered together in the archives of the Society of Finnish Literature at Helsingfors is imposing in bulk and of great importance to the student of comparative folklore.

My own excursions into the Finnish have been made possible through the kindness and endless patience of my friend, Lydia Tulonen (Mrs. Kurt J. Rahlson). With her as a native guide I have been wandering some time through the byways of Finnish folklore. The present volume is the traveler's pack I have brought home with me filled with strange treasures which will, I hope, seem as lovely to others as they seemed to me when first I came upon them.

The stories as I offer them are not translations but my own versions. Literal translations from the Finnish would make small appeal to the general reader. To English ears the Finnish is stiff, bald, and monotonous. One has only to read or attempt to read Kirby's excellent translation of the *Kalevala* to realize the truth of this statement. So I make no apology for retelling these tales in a manner more likely to prove entertaining to the English reader, whether child or adult.

NOTE ix

In some form or other all the tales in this book may be found in the various folklore collections made by Eero Salmelainen, one of the patriotic young scholars who followed in Lönnrot's footsteps. His books were sponsored by the Society of Finnish Literature and used in its campaign to bring back the Finnish language to the Finns at a time when Swedish was the official language of the country.

Full of local color as these stories are, it would be vain to pretend that they are not, for the most part, variants of stories told the world over. All that I can claim for them is that they are dramatic and picturesque, that they are told with a wealth of charming detail which is essentially Finnish, and that they are certainly new to the generality of English readers. *The Three Chests,* so characteristic in feeling of a country famous for its lakes and marshes, is the variant of a German story which Grimm gives as *Fitcher's Bird.* Of *The Forest Bride* I have found variants in the folklore of many lands. There are several very beautiful ones in the Russian; in other books I myself have retold two, one current among the Czechs and one among the Serbians; Grimm has two different versions in *The Three Feathers* and *The Poor Miller's Boy and the Cat;* and Madame d'Aulnoy has used the same story in her elaborate tale, *The White Cat*. There is a well-known Oriental version of *Mighty Mikko* in which the part of the fox is played by a jackal and I am sure that Mikko's faithful retainer, though neither city-bred nor polished, is after all pretty closely related to that most debonnaire of Frenchmen, *Puss in Boots*. Perrault probably and Madame d'Aulnoy certainly are in turn indebted to Straparola. And so it goes.

The little cycle of animal stories included under *Mikko the Fox* will of course instantly invite comparison with the Beast Epic of *Reynard the Fox*. The two have many episodes in common and both have episodes to be found in Æsop and in those books of animal analogues, widely read in mediæval times, *Physiologus* and the *Disciplina Clericalis* of Petrus Alfonsus. The *Reynard* as we have it is a finished satire on church and state and in its present form has been current in Europe since the twelfth century. It was thought at one time that the animal stories found in Finland were debased versions of the *Reynard* stories, but scholars are now of opinion that they antedate *Reynard* and are similar to the earlier simpler stories upon which the *Reynard* cycle was originally built. This makes the little Finnish tales of great interest to the student. Needless to say I do not present them for this reason but because they

NOTE

seem to me charming merely as fables. The animals here are not the clerics and the judges and the nobles that the *Reynard* animals are, but plain downright Finnish peasants, sometimes stupid, often dull, frequently amusing, and always very human.

I have taken one liberty with spelling. I have transliterated Syöjätär, the name of the dread Finnish witch, as Suyettar. I have been unwilling to translate by the insufficient word, *bath-house* or *vapor bath,* that very characteristic institution of Finnish family life, the *sauna,* but have retained the Finnish word, *sauna,* allowing the context in each case to indicate the meaning.

P. F.

New York
June 19, 1922

CONTENTS

	PAGE
THE TRUE BRIDE: The Story of Ilona and the King's Son	1
MIGHTY MIKKO: The Story of a Poor Woodsman and a Grateful Fox	25
THE THREE CHESTS: The Story of the Wicked Old Man of the Sea	47
LOG: The Story of the Hero Who Released the Sun	67
THE LITTLE SISTER: The Story of Suyettar and the Nine Brothers	99
THE FOREST BRIDE: The Story of a Little Mouse Who was a Princess	121
THE ENCHANTED GROUSE: The Story of Helli and the Little Locked Box	141
THE TERRIBLE OLLI: The Story of an Honest Finn and a Wicked Troll	155
THE DEVIL'S HIDE: The Story of the Boy Who Wouldn't Lose His Temper	171

CONTENTS

		PAGE
THE MYSTERIOUS SERVANT: The Story of a Young Man Who Respected the Dead		193
FAMILIAR FACES:		
I	Mary, Mary, So Contrary!	209
II	Jane, Jane, Don't Complain!	215
III	Susan Walker, What a Talker!	221
MIKKO THE FOX: A Nursery Epic in Sixteen Adventures		
I	The Animals Take a Bite	229
II	The Partners	235
III	The Fox and the Crow	243
IV	The Chief Mourner	251
V	Mirri, the Cat	257
VI	The Fox's Servant	263
VII	The Wolf Sings	267
VIII	The Clever Goat	273
IX	The Harvest	279
X	The Porridge	283
XI	Nurse Mikko	287
XII	The Bear Says *North*	293
XIII	Osmo's Share	297
XIV	The Reward of Kindness	301
XV	The Bear and the Mouse	307
XVI	The Last of Osmo	309

FULL-PAGE ILLUSTRATIONS

Ilona came floating up through the waves . . . *Frontispiece*	
	PAGE
The old king snake has wound himself around Osmo's arm .	15
The King thought that if Mikko should see his daughter .	33
She fitted the key in the lock	57
"This last and mightiest battle is for me!"	85
Suyettar bewitching Kerttu	111
She beckoned to Veikko	135
On it flew until it reached the broad Ocean	147
Olli and the Troll's horse	161
From the bones of the cattle he laid three bridges . . .	183
"She is under an evil enchantment and I am delivering her!"	203
When she got to the middle of the stream	208
They were so busy eating and drinking	214
They carried home the treasure on their backs . . .	220
Osmo, the Bear, grunted out: "Huh! That's easy! We'll eat the smallest of us next!"	228

ILLUSTRATIONS

	PAGE
"Wake up, Pekka! Wake up! There's butter running out of your nose!"	239
"I'll teach that Crow to interfere with my affairs!" the Fox muttered to himself as he trotted off	249
And Mikko, beginning with a little whimpering sound, slowly rose to a high heartrending cry	253
He jerked quickly away and fled and the Bear was left standing with his mouth wide open	259
A terrible creature landed on his nose and drove it full of pins and needles	262
The Wolf went staggering around the room howling at the top of his voice	269
In the confusion that followed the Wolves stampeded, running helter-skelter in all directions	272
"Here are three of us and, see, here on the floor is our harvest already divided into three heaps"	278
He dropped it in the water and of course it spread out far and wide and the current carried it off	282
He ran after Mikko and was about to overtake him when Mikko slipped into a crevice in the rocks. Only one paw stuck out	289
Of course the instant he opened his mouth, the Grouse flew away	292
"Why, do you know," he said, "my turnips and my bread don't taste a bit like this!"	296
The first person they met was an old Horse. They put their case to him	300
With that the Bear lifted his paw and the little Mouse scampered off	306
So that was the End	315

THE TRUE BRIDE

The Story of Ilona and the King's Son

THE TRUE BRIDE

There were once two orphans, a brother and a sister, who lived alone in the old farmhouse where their fathers before them had lived for many generations. The brother's name was Osmo, the sister's Ilona. Osmo was an industrious youth, but the farm was small and barren and he was hard put to it to make a livelihood.

"Sister," he said one day, "I think it might be well if I went out into the world and found work."

"Do as you think best, brother," Ilona said. "I'm sure I can manage on here alone."

So Osmo started off, promising to come back for his sister as soon as he could give her a new home. He wandered far and wide and at last got employment from the King's Son as a shepherd.

The King's Son was about Osmo's age, and often when he met Osmo tending his flocks he would stop and talk to him.

One day Osmo told the King's Son about his sister, Ilona.

"I have wandered far over the face of the earth," he said, "and never have I seen so beautiful a maiden as Ilona."

"What does she look like?" the King's Son asked.

Osmo drew a picture of her and she seemed to the King's Son so beautiful that at once he fell in love with her.

"Osmo," he said, "if you will go home and get your sister, I will marry her."

So Osmo hurried home not by the long land route by which he had come but straight over the water in a boat.

"Sister," he cried, as soon as he saw Ilona, "you must come with me at once for the King's Son wishes to marry you!"

He thought Ilona would be overjoyed, but she sighed and shook her head.

"What is it, sister? Why do you sigh?"

"Because it grieves me to leave this old house where our fathers have lived for so many generations."

"Nonsense, Ilona! What is this little old house compared to the King's castle where you will live once you marry the King's Son!"

But Ilona only shook her head.

"It's no use, brother! I can't bear to leave this old house until the grindstone with which our fathers for generations ground their meal is worn out."

When Osmo found she was firm, he went secretly and broke the old grindstone into small pieces. He then put the pieces together so that the stone looked the same as before. But of course the next time Ilona touched it, it fell apart.

"Now, sister, you'll come, will you not?" Osmo asked.

But again Ilona shook her head.

"It's no use, brother. I can't bear to go until the old stool where our mothers have sat spinning these many generations is worn through."

So again Osmo took things into his own hands and going secretly to the old spinning stool he broke it and when Ilona sat on it again it fell to pieces.

Then Ilona said she couldn't go until the old mortar which had been in use for generations should fall to bits at a blow from the pestle. Osmo cracked the mortar and the next time Ilona struck it with the pestle it broke.

Then Ilona said she couldn't go until the old worn doorsill over which so many of their forefathers had walked should fall to splinters at the brush of her skirts. So Osmo secretly split the old doorsill into thin slivers and, when next Ilona stepped over it, the brush of her skirts sent the splinters flying.

"I see now I must go," Ilona said, "for the house of our forefathers no longer holds me."

So she packed all her ribbons and her bodices and skirts in a bright wooden box and, calling her little dog Pilka, she stepped into the boat and Osmo rowed her off in the direction of the King's castle.

Soon they passed a long narrow spit of land at the end of which stood a woman waving her arms. That is she looked like a woman. Really she was Suyettar but they, of course, did not know this.

"Take me in your boat!" she cried.

"Shall we?" Osmo asked his sister.

"I don't think we ought to," Ilona said. "We don't know who she is or what she wants and she may be evil."

So Osmo rowed on. But the woman kept shouting: "Hi, there! Take me in your boat! Take me!"

A second time Osmo paused and asked his sister:

"Don't you think we ought to take her?"

"No," Ilona said.

So Osmo rowed on again. At this the creature raised

such a pitiful outcry demanding what they meant denying assistance to a poor woman that Osmo was unable longer to refuse and in spite of Ilona's warning he rowed to land.

Suyettar instantly jumped into the boat and seated herself in the middle with her face towards Osmo and her back towards Ilona.

"What a fine young man!" Suyettar said in whining flattering tones. "See how strong he is at the oars! And what a beautiful girl, too! I daresay the King's Son would fall in love with her if ever he saw her!"

Thereupon Osmo very foolishly told Suyettar that the King's Son had already promised to marry Ilona. At that an evil look came into Suyettar's face and she sat silent for a time biting her fingers. Then she began mumbling a spell that made Osmo deaf to what Ilona was saying and Ilona deaf to what Osmo was saying.

At last in the distance the towers of the King's castle appeared.

"Stand up, sister!" Osmo said. "Shake out your skirts and arrange your pretty ribbons! We'll soon be landing now!"

Ilona could see her brother's lips moving but of course she could not hear what he was saying.

"What is it, brother?" she asked.

Suyettar answered for him:

"Osmo orders you to jump headlong into the water!"

"No! No!" Ilona cried. "He couldn't order anything so cruel as that!"

Presently Osmo said:

"Sister, what ails you? Don't you hear me? Shake out your skirts and arrange your pretty ribbons for we'll soon be landing now."

"What is it, brother?" Ilona asked.

As before Suyettar answered for him:

"Osmo orders you to jump headlong into the water!"

"Brother, how can you order so cruel a thing!" Ilona cried, bursting into tears. "Is it for this you made me leave the home of my fathers?"

A third time Osmo said:

"Stand up, sister, and shake out your skirts and arrange your ribbons! We'll soon be landing now!"

"I can't hear you, brother! What is it you say?"

Suyettar turned on her fiercely and screamed:

"Osmo orders you to jump headlong into the water!"

"If he says I must, I must!" poor Ilona sobbed, and with that she leapt overboard.

Osmo tried to save her but Suyettar held him back

and with her own arms rowed off and Ilona was left to sink.

"What will become of me now!" Osmo cried. "When the King's Son finds I have not brought him my sister he will surely order my death!"

"Not at all!" Suyettar said. "Do as I say and no harm will come to you. Offer me to the King's Son and tell him I am your sister. He won't know the difference and anyway I'm sure I'm just as beautiful as Ilona ever was!"

With that Suyettar opened the wooden box that held Ilona's clothes and helped herself to skirt and bodice and gay colored ribbons. She decked herself out in these and for a little while she really did succeed in looking like a pretty young girl.

So Osmo presented Suyettar to the King's Son as Ilona, and the King's Son because he had given his word married her. But before one day was past, he called Osmo to him and asked him angrily:

"What did you mean by telling me your sister was beautiful?"

"Isn't she beautiful?" Osmo faltered.

"No! I thought she was at first but she isn't! She is ugly and evil and you shall pay the penalty for having deceived me!"

Thereupon he ordered that Osmo be shut up in a place filled with serpents.

"If you are innocent," the King's Son said, "the serpents will not harm you. If you are guilty they will devour you!"

Meanwhile poor Ilona when she jumped into the water sank down, down, down, until she reached the Sea King's palace. They received her kindly there and comforted her and the Sea King's Son, touched by her grief and beauty, offered to marry her. But Ilona was homesick for the upper world and would not listen to him.

"I want to see my brother again!" she wept.

They told her that the King's Son had thrown her brother to the serpents and had married Suyettar in her stead, but Ilona still begged so pitifully to be allowed to return to earth that at last the Sea King said:

"Very well, then! For three successive nights I will allow you to return to the upper world. But after that never again!"

So they decked Ilona in the lovely jewels of the sea with great strands of pearls about her neck and to each of her ankles they attached long silver chains. As she rose in the water the sound of the chains was like the chiming of silver bells and could be heard for five miles.

Ilona came to the surface of the water just where Osmo had landed. The first thing she saw was his boat at the water's edge and curled up asleep in the bottom of the boat her own little dog, Pilka.

"Pilka!" Ilona cried, and the little dog woke with a bark of joy and licked Ilona's hand and yelped and frisked.

Then Ilona sang this magic song to Pilka:

> "Peely, peely, Pilka, pide,
> Lift the latch and slip inside!
> Past the watchdog in the yard,
> Past the sleeping men on guard!
> Creep in softly as a snake,
> Then creep out before they wake!
> Peely, peely, Pilka, pide,
> Peely, peely, Pilka!"

Pilka barked and frisked and said:

"Yes, mistress, yes! I'll do whatever you bid me!"

Ilona gave the little dog an embroidered square of gold and silver which she herself had worked down in the Sea King's palace.

"Take this," she said to Pilka, "and put it on the pillow where the King's Son lies asleep. Perhaps when he sees it he will know that it comes from Osmo's true sister and that the frightful creature he has married is Suyettar. Then perhaps he will release Osmo before the serpents devour him. Go now, my faithful Pilka, and come back to me before the dawn."

So Pilka raced off to the King's palace carrying the square of embroidery in her teeth. Ilona waited and half an hour before sunrise the little dog came panting back.

"What news, Pilka? How fares my brother and how is my poor love, the King's Son?"

"Osmo is still with the serpents," Pilka answered, "but they haven't eaten him yet. I left the embroidered square on the pillow where the King's Son's head was lying. Suyettar was asleep on the bed beside him where you should be, dear mistress. Suyettar's awful mouth was open and she was snoring horribly. The King's Son moved uneasily for he was troubled even in his sleep."

"And did you go through the castle, Pilka?"

"Yes, dear mistress."

"And did you see the remains of the wedding feast?"

"Yes, dear mistress, the remains of a feast that shamed the King's Son, for Suyettar served bones instead of meat, fish heads, turnip tops, and bread burned to a cinder."

"Good Pilka!" Ilona said. "Good little dog! You have done well! Now the dawn is coming and I must go back to the Sea King's palace. But I shall come again to-night and also to-morrow night and do you be here waiting for me."

Pilka promised and Ilona sank down into the sea to a clanking of chains that sounded like silver bells. The King's Son heard them in his sleep and for a moment woke and said:

"What's that?"

"What's what?" snarled Suyettar. "You're dreaming! Go back to sleep!"

A few hours later when he woke again, he found the lovely square of embroidery on his pillow.

"Who made this?" he cried.

Suyettar was busy combing her snaky locks. She turned on him quickly.

"Who made what?"

When she saw the embroidery she tried to snatch it from him, but he held it tight.

"I made it, of course!" she declared. "Who but me would sit up all night and work while you lay snoring!"

But the King's Son, as he folded the embroidery, muttered to himself:

"It doesn't look to me much like your work!"

After he had breakfasted, the King's Son asked for news of Osmo. A slave was sent to the place of the serpents and when he returned he reported that Osmo was sitting amongst them uninjured.

"The old king snake has made friends with him," he added, "and has wound himself around Osmo's arm."

The King's Son was amazed at this news and also relieved, for the whole affair troubled him sorely and he was beginning to suspect a mystery.

He knew an old wise woman who lived alone in a little hut on the seashore and he decided he would go and consult her. So he went to her and told her about Osmo and how Osmo had deceived him in regard to his sister. Then he told her how the serpents instead of devouring Osmo had made friends with him and last he showed her the square of lovely embroidery he had found on his pillow that morning.

"There is a mystery somewhere, granny," he said in conclusion, "and I know not how to solve it."

The old woman looked at him thoughtfully.

"My son," she said at last, "that is never Osmo's sister that you have married. Take an old woman's word—it is Suyettar! Yet Osmo's sister must be alive and the embroidery must be a token from her. It

The old king snake has wound himself around Osmo's arm

probably means that she begs you to release her brother."

"Suyettar!" repeated the King's Son, aghast.

At first he couldn't believe such a horrible thing possible and yet that, if it were so, would explain much.

"I wonder if you're right," he said. "I must be on my guard!"

That night on the stroke of midnight to the sound of silver chimes Ilona came floating up through the waves and little Pilka, as she appeared, greeted her with barks of joy.

As before Ilona sang:

> "Peely, peely, Pilka, pide,
> Lift the latch and slip inside!
> Past the watchdog in the yard,
> Past the sleeping men on guard!
> Creep in softly as a snake,
> Then creep out before they wake!
> Peely, peely, Pilka, pide,
> Peely, peely, Pilka!"

This time Ilona gave Pilka a shirt for the King's Son. Beautifully embroidered it was in gold and silver and Ilona herself had worked it in the Sea King's palace.

Pilka carried it safely to the castle and left it on the

pillow where the King's Son could see it as soon as he woke. Then Pilka visited the place of the serpents and before the first ray of dawn was back at the seashore to reassure Ilona of Osmo's safety.

Then dawn came and Ilona, as she sank in the waves to the chime of silver bells, called out to Pilka:

"Meet me here to-night at the same hour! Fail me not, dear Pilka, for to-night is the last night that the Sea King will allow me to come to the upper world!"

Pilka, howling with grief, made promise:

"I'll be here, dear mistress, that I will!"

The King's Son that morning, as he opened his eyes, saw the embroidered shirt lying on the pillow at his head. He thought at first he must be dreaming for it was more beautiful than any shirt that had ever been worked by human fingers.

"Ah!" he sighed at last, "who made this?"

"Who made what?" Suyettar demanded rudely.

When she saw the shirt she tried to snatch it, but the King's Son held it from her. Then she pretended to laugh and said:

"Oh, that! I made it, of course! Do you think any one else in the world would sit up all night and work for you while you lie there snoring! And small thanks I get for it, too!"

"It doesn't look to me like your work!" said the King's Son significantly.

Again the slave reported to him that Osmo was alive and unhurt by the serpents.

"Strange!" thought the King's Son.

He took the embroidered shirt and made the old wise woman another visit.

"Ah!" she said, when she saw the shirt, "now I understand! Listen, my Prince: last night at midnight I was awakened by the chime of silver bells and I got up and looked out the door. Just there at the water's edge, close to that little boat, I saw a strange sight. A lovely maiden rose from the waves holding in her hands the very shirt that you now have. A little dog that was lying in the boat greeted her with barks of joy. She sang a magic rime to the dog and gave it the shirt and off it ran. That maid, my Prince, must be Ilona. She must be in the Sea King's power and I think she is begging you to rescue her and to release her brother."

The King's Son slowly nodded his head.

"Granny, I'm sure what you say is true! Help me to rescue Ilona and I shall reward you richly."

"Then, my son, you must act at once, for to-night, I heard Ilona say, is the last night that the Sea King will allow her to come to the upper world. Go now to the smith and have him forge you a strong iron chain and a great strong scythe. Then to-night hide you down yonder in the shadow of the boat. At midnight when you hear the silver chimes and the maiden slowly rises from the waves, throw the iron chain about her and quickly draw her to you. Then, with one sweep of your scythe, cut the silver chains that are fastened to her ankles. But remember, my son, that is not all. She is under enchantment and as you try to grasp her the Sea King will change her to many things—a fish, a bird, a fly, and I know not what, and if in any form she escape you, then all is lost."

At once the King's Son hurried away to the smithy and had the smith forge him a strong iron chain and a heavy sharp scythe. Then when night fell he hid in the shadow of the boat and waited. Pilka snuggled up beside him. Midnight came and to the sweet chiming as of silver bells Ilona slowly rose from the waves. As she came she began singing:

"Peely, peely, Pilka, pide———"

Instantly the King's Son threw the strong iron chain about her and drew her to him. Then with one mighty sweep of the scythe he severed the silver chains that were attached to her ankles and the silver chains fell chiming into the depths. Another instant and the maiden in his arms was no maiden but a slimy fish that squirmed and wriggled and almost slipped through his fingers. He killed the fish and, lo! it was not a fish but a frightened bird that struggled to escape. He killed the bird and, lo! it was not a bird but a writhing lizard. And so on through many transformations, growing finally small and weak until at last there was only a mosquito. He crushed this and in his arms he found again the lovely Ilona.

"Ah, dear one," he said, "you are my true bride and not Suyettar who pretended she was you! Come, we will go at once to the castle and confront her!"

But Ilona cried out at this:

"Not there, my Prince, not there! Suyettar if she saw me would kill me and devour me! Keep me from her!"

"Very well, my dear one," the King's Son said. "We'll wait until to-morrow and after to-morrow there will be no Suyettar to fear."

So for that night they took shelter in the old wise woman's hut, Ilona and the King's Son and faithful little Pilka.

The next morning early the King's Son returned to

the castle and had the *sauna* heated. Just inside the door he had a deep hole dug and filled it with burning tar. Then over the top of the hole he stretched a brown mat and on the brown mat a blue mat. When all was ready he went indoors and roused Suyettar.

"Where have you been all night?" she demanded angrily.

"Forgive me this time," he begged in pretended humility, "and I promise never again to be parted from my own true bride. Come now, my dear, and bathe for the *sauna* is ready."

Then Suyettar, who loved to have people see her go to the *sauna* just as if she were a real human being, put on a long bathrobe and clapped her hands. Four slaves appeared. Two took up the train of her bathrobe and the two others supported her on either side. Slowly she marched out of the castle, across the courtyard, and over to the *sauna*.

"They all really think I'm a human princess!" she said to herself, and she was so sure she was beautiful and admired that she tossed her head and smirked from side to side and took little mincing steps.

When she reached the *sauna* she was ready to drop the bathrobe and jump over the doorsill to the steaming shelf, but the King's Son whispered:

THE TRUE BRIDGE

"Nay! Nay! Remember your dignity as a beautiful princess and walk over the blue mat!"

So with one more toss of her head, one more smirk of her ugly face, Suyettar stepped on the blue mat and sank into the hole of burning tar. Then the King's Son quickly locked the door of the *sauna* and left her there to burn in the tar, for burning, you know, is the only way to destroy Suyettar. As she burned the last hateful thing Suyettar did was to tear out handfuls of her hair and scatter them broadcast in the air.

"Let these," she cried, yelling and cursing, "turn into mosquitos and worms and moths and trouble mankind forever!"

Then her yells grew fainter and at last ceased altogether and the King's Son knew that it was now safe to bring Ilona home. First, however, he had Osmo released from the place of the serpents and asked his forgiveness for the unjust punishment.

Then he and Osmo together went to the hut of the old wise woman and there with tears of happiness the brother and sister were reunited. The King's Son to show his gratitude to the old wise woman begged her to accompany them to the castle and presently they all set forth with Pilka frisking ahead and barking for joy.

That day there was a new wedding feast spread at the castle and this time it was not bones and fish heads and burnt crusts but such food as the King's Son had not tasted for many a day.

To celebrate his happy marriage the King's Son made Osmo his chamberlain and gave Pilka a beautiful new collar.

"Now at last," Ilona said, "I am glad I left the house of my forefathers."

MIGHTY MIKKO

The Story of a Poor Woodsman and a Grateful Fox

MIGHTY MIKKO

There was once an old woodsman and his wife who had an only son named Mikko. As the mother lay dying the young man wept bitterly.

"When you are gone, my dear mother," he said, "there will be no one left to think of me."

The poor woman comforted him as best she could and said to him:

"You will still have your father."

Shortly after the woman's death, the old man, too, was taken ill.

"Now, indeed, I shall be left desolate and alone," Mikko thought, as he sat beside his father's bedside and saw him grow weaker and weaker.

"My boy," the old man said just before he died, "I have nothing to leave you but the three snares with which these many years I have caught wild animals. Those snares now belong to you. When I am dead, go into the woods and if you find a wild creature caught in any of them, free it gently and bring it home alive."

After his father's death, Mikko remembered the snares and went out to the woods to see them. The first was empty and also the second, but in the third he found a little red Fox. He carefully lifted the spring that had shut down on one of the Fox's feet and then carried the little creature home in his arms. He shared his supper with it and when he lay down to sleep the Fox curled up at his feet. They lived together some time until they became close friends.

"Mikko," said the Fox one day, "why are you so sad?"

"Because I'm lonely."

"Pooh!" said the Fox. "That's no way for a young man to talk! You ought to get married! Then you wouldn't feel lonely!"

"Married!" Mikko repeated. "How can I get married? I can't marry a poor girl because I'm too poor myself and a rich girl wouldn't marry me."

"Nonsense!" said the Fox. "You're a fine well set up young man and you're kind and gentle. What more could a princess ask?"

Mikko laughed to think of a princess wanting him for a husband.

"I mean what I say!" the Fox insisted. "Take our own Princess now. What would you think of marrying her?"

Mikko laughed louder than before.

"I have heard," he said, "that she is the most beautiful princess in the world! Any man would be happy to marry her!"

"Very well," the Fox said, "if you feel that way about her then I'll arrange the wedding for you."

With that the little Fox actually did trot off to the royal castle and gain audience with the King.

"My master sends you greetings," the Fox said, "and he begs you to loan him your bushel measure."

"My bushel measure!" the King repeated in surprise. "Who is your master and why does he want my bushel measure?"

"Ssh!" the Fox whispered as though he didn't want the courtiers to hear what he was saying. Then slipping up quite close to the King he murmured in his ear:

"Surely you have heard of Mikko, haven't you?—Mighty Mikko as he's called."

The King had never heard of any Mikko who was known as Mighty Mikko but, thinking that perhaps he should have heard of him, he shook his head and murmured:

"H'm! Mikko! Mighty Mikko! Oh, to be sure! Yes, yes, of course!"

"My master is about to start off on a journey and he needs a bushel measure for a very particular reason."

"I understand! I understand!" the King said, although he didn't understand at all, and he gave orders that the bushel measure which they used in the storeroom of the castle be brought in and given to the Fox.

The Fox carried off the measure and hid it in the woods. Then he scurried about to all sorts of little out of the way nooks and crannies where people had hidden their savings and he dug up a gold piece here and a silver piece there until he had a handful. Then he went back to the woods and stuck the various coins in the cracks of the measure. The next day he returned to the King.

"My master, Mighty Mikko," he said, "sends you thanks, O King, for the use of your bushel measure."

The King held out his hand and when the Fox gave him the measure he peeped inside to see if by chance it contained any trace of what had recently been measured. His eye of course at once caught the glint of the gold and silver coins lodged in the cracks.

"Ah!" he said, thinking Mikko must be a very mighty lord indeed to be so careless of his wealth; "I should like to meet your master. Won't you and he come and visit me?"

This was what the Fox wanted the King to say but he pretended to hesitate.

"I thank your Majesty for the kind invitation," he said, "but I fear my master can't accept it just now. He wants to get married soon and we are about to start off on a long journey to inspect a number of foreign princesses."

This made the King all the more anxious to have Mikko visit him at once for he thought that if Mikko should see his daughter before he saw those foreign princesses he might fall in love with her and marry her. So he said to the Fox:

"My dear fellow, you must prevail on your master to make me a visit before he starts out on his travels! You will, won't you?"

The Fox looked this way and that as if he were too embarrassed to speak.

"Your Majesty," he said at last, "I pray you pardon my frankness. The truth is you are not rich enough to entertain my master and your castle isn't big enough to house the immense retinue that always attends him."

The King, who by this time was frantic to see Mikko, lost his head completely.

"My dear Fox," he said, "I'll give you anything in the world if you prevail upon your master to visit me at once! Couldn't you suggest to him to travel with a modest retinue this time?"

The Fox shook his head.

"No. His rule is either to travel with a great retinue or to go on foot disguised as a poor woodsman attended only by me."

"Couldn't you prevail on him to come to me disguised as a poor woodsman?" the King begged. "Once he was here, I could place gorgeous clothes at his disposal."

But still the Fox shook his head.

"I fear Your Majesty's wardrobe doesn't contain the kind of clothes my master is accustomed to."

"I assure you I've got some very good clothes," the King said. "Come along this minute and we'll go through them and I'm sure you'll find some that your master would wear."

So they went to a room which was like a big wardrobe with hundreds and hundreds of hooks upon which were hung hundreds of coats and breeches and embroidered shirts. The King ordered his attendants to bring the costumes down one by one and place them before the Fox.

The King thought that if Mikko should see his daughter

They began with the plainer clothes.

"Good enough for most people," the Fox said, "but not for my master."

Then they took down garments of a finer grade.

"I'm afraid you're going to all this trouble for nothing," the Fox said. "Frankly now, don't you realize that my master couldn't possibly put on any of these things!"

The King, who had hoped to keep for his own use his most gorgeous clothes of all, now ordered these to be shown.

The Fox looked at them sideways, sniffed them critically, and at last said:

"Well, perhaps my master would consent to wear these for a few days. They are not what he is accustomed to wear but I will say this for him: he is not proud."

The King was overjoyed.

"Very well, my dear Fox, I'll have the guest chambers put in readiness for your master's visit and I'll have all these, my finest clothes, laid out for him. You won't disappoint me, will you?"

"I'll do my best," the Fox promised.

With that he bade the King a civil good day and ran home to Mikko.

The next day as the Princess was peeping out of an upper window of the castle, she saw a young woodsman approaching accompanied by a Fox. He was a fine stalwart youth and the Princess, who knew from the presence of the Fox that he must be Mikko, gave a long sigh and confided to her serving maid:

"I think I could fall in love with that young man if he really were only a woodsman!"

Later when she saw him arrayed in her father's finest clothes—which looked so well on Mikko that no one even recognized them as the King's—she lost her heart completely and when Mikko was presented to her she blushed and trembled just as any ordinary girl might before a handsome young man.

All the Court was equally delighted with Mikko. The ladies went into ecstasies over his modest manners, his fine figure, and the gorgeousness of his clothes, and the old graybeard Councilors, nodding their heads in approval, said to each other:

"Nothing of the coxcomb about this young fellow! In spite of his great wealth see how politely he listens to us when we talk!"

The next day the Fox went privately to the King, and said:

"My master is a man of few words and quick judgment. He bids me tell you that your daughter, the Princess, pleases him mightily and that, with your approval, he will make his addresses to her at once."

The King was greatly agitated and began:

"My dear Fox—"

But the Fox interrupted him to say:

"Think the matter over carefully and give me your decision to-morrow."

So the King consulted with the Princess and with his Councilors and in a short time the marriage was arranged and the wedding ceremony actually performed!

"Didn't I tell you?" the Fox said, when he and Mikko were alone after the wedding.

"Yes," Mikko acknowledged, "you did promise that I should marry the Princess. But, tell me, now that I am married what am I to do? I can't live on here forever with my wife."

"Put your mind at rest," the Fox said. "I've thought of everything. Just do as I tell you and you'll have nothing to regret. To-night say to the King: 'It is now only fitting that you should visit me and see for yourself the sort of castle over which your daughter is hereafter to be mistress!'"

When Mikko said this to the King, the King was

overjoyed for now that the marriage had actually taken place he was wondering whether he hadn't perhaps been a little hasty. Mikko's words reassured him and he eagerly accepted the invitation.

On the morrow the Fox said to Mikko:

"Now I'll run on ahead and get things ready for you."

"But where are you going?" Mikko said, frightened at the thought of being deserted by his little friend.

The Fox drew Mikko aside and whispered softly:

"A few days' march from here there is a very gorgeous castle belonging to a wicked old dragon who is known as the Worm. I think the Worm's castle would just about suit you."

"I'm sure it would," Mikko agreed. "But how are we to get it away from the Worm?"

"Trust me," the Fox said. "All you need do is this: lead the King and his courtiers along the main highway until by noon to-morrow you reach a crossroads. Turn there to the left and go straight on until you see the tower of the Worm's castle. If you meet any men by the wayside, shepherds or the like, ask them whose men they are and show no surprise at their answer. So now, dear master, farewell until we meet again at your beautiful castle."

The little Fox trotted off at a smart pace and Mikko and the Princess and the King attended by the whole Court followed in more leisurely fashion.

The little Fox, when he had left the main highway at the crossroads, soon met ten woodsmen with axes over their shoulders. They were all dressed in blue smocks of the same cut.

"Good day," the Fox said politely. "Whose men are you?"

"Our master is known as the Worm," the woodsmen told him.

"My poor, poor lads!" the Fox said, shaking his head sadly.

"What's the matter?" the woodsmen asked.

For a few moments the Fox pretended to be too overcome with emotion to speak. Then he said:

"My poor lads, don't you know that the King is coming with a great force to destroy the Worm and all his people?"

The woodsmen were simple fellows and this news threw them into great consternation.

"Is there no way for us to escape?" they asked.

The Fox put his paw to his head and thought.

"Well," he said at last, "there is one way you might escape and that is by telling every one who asks you that you are the Mighty Mikko's men. But if you value your lives never again say that your master is the Worm."

"We are Mighty Mikko's men!" the woodsmen at once began repeating over and over. "We are Mighty Mikko's men!"

A little farther on the road the Fox met twenty grooms, dressed in the same blue smocks, who were tending a hundred beautiful horses. The Fox talked to the twenty grooms as he had talked to the woodsmen and before he left them they, too, were shouting:

"We are Mighty Mikko's men!"

Next the Fox came to a huge flock of a thousand sheep tended by thirty shepherds all dressed in the Worm's blue smocks. He stopped and talked to them until he had them roaring out:

"We are Mighty Mikko's men!"

Then the Fox trotted on until he reached the castle of the Worm. He found the Worm himself inside lolling lazily about. He was a huge dragon and had been a great warrior in his day. In fact his castle and his lands and his servants and his possessions had all been won in battle. But now for many years no one had cared to fight him and he had grown fat and lazy.

"Good day," the Fox said, pretending to be very

breathless and frightened. "You're the Worm, aren't you?"

"Yes," the dragon said, boastfully, "I am the great Worm!"

The Fox pretended to grow more agitated.

"My poor fellow, I am sorry for you! But of course none of us can expect to live forever. Well, I must hurry along. I thought I would just stop and say good-by."

Made uneasy by the Fox's words, the Worm cried out:

"Wait just a minute! What's the matter?"

The Fox was already at the door but at the Worm's entreaty he paused and said over his shoulder:

"Why, my poor fellow, you surely know, don't you? that the King with a great force is coming to destroy you and all your people!"

"What!" the Worm gasped, turning a sickly green with fright. He knew he was fat and helpless and could never again fight as in the years gone by.

"Don't go just yet!" he begged the Fox. "When is the King coming?"

"He's on the highway now! That's why I must be going! Good-by!"

"My dear Fox, stay just a moment and I'll reward

you richly! Help me to hide so that the King won't find me! What about the shed where the linen is stored? I could crawl under the linen and then if you locked the door from the outside the King could never find me."

"Very well," the Fox agreed, "but we must hurry!"

So they ran outside to the shed where the linen was kept and the Worm hid himself under the linen. The Fox locked the door, then set fire to the shed, and soon there was nothing left of that wicked old dragon, the Worm, but a handful of ashes.

The Fox now called together the dragon's household and talked them over to Mikko as he had the woodsmen and the grooms and the shepherds.

Meanwhile the King and his party were slowly covering the ground over which the Fox had sped so quickly. When they came to the ten woodsmen in blue smocks, the King said:

"I wonder whose woodsmen those are."

One of his attendants asked the woodsmen and the ten of them shouted out at the top of their voices:

"We are Mighty Mikko's men!"

Mikko said nothing and the King and all the Court were impressed anew with his modesty.

A little farther on they met the twenty grooms with

their hundred prancing horses. When the grooms were questioned, they answered with a shout:

"We are Mighty Mikko's men!"

"The Fox certainly spoke the truth," the King thought to himself, "when he told me of Mikko's riches!"

A little later the thirty shepherds when they were questioned made answer in a chorus that was deafening to hear:

"We are Mighty Mikko's men!"

The sight of the thousand sheep that belonged to his son-in-law made the King feel poor and humble in comparison and the courtiers whispered among themselves:

"For all his simple manner, Mighty Mikko must be a richer, more powerful lord than the King himself! In fact it is only a very great lord indeed who could be so simple!"

At last they reached the castle which from the blue smocked soldiers that guarded the gateway they knew to be Mikko's. The Fox came out to welcome the King's party and behind him in two rows all the household servants. These, at a signal from the Fox, cried out in one voice:

"We are Mighty Mikko's men!"

Then Mikko in the same simple manner that he would have used in his father's mean little hut in the woods bade the King and his followers welcome and they all entered the castle where they found a great feast already prepared and waiting.

The King stayed on for several days and the more he saw of Mikko the better pleased he was that he had him for a son-in-law.

When he was leaving he said to Mikko:

"Your castle is so much grander than mine that I hesitate ever asking you back for a visit."

But Mikko reassured the King by saying earnestly:

"My dear father-in-law, when first I entered your castle I thought it was the most beautiful castle in the world!"

The King was flattered and the courtiers whispered among themselves:

'How affable of him to say that when he knows very well how much grander his own castle is!"

When the King and his followers were safely gone, the little red Fox came to Mikko and said:

"Now, my master, you have no reason to feel sad and lonely. You are lord of the most beautiful castle in the world and you have for wife a sweet and lovely Princess. You have no longer any need of me, so I am going to bid you farewell."

Mikko thanked the little Fox for all he had done and the little Fox trotted off to the woods.

So you see that Mikko's poor old father, although he had no wealth to leave his son, was really the cause of all Mikko's good fortune, for it was he who told Mikko in the first place to carry home alive anything he might find caught in the snares.

THE THREE CHESTS

The Story of the Wicked Old Man of the Sea

THE THREE CHESTS

There was once an honest old farmer who had three daughters. His farm ran down to the shores of a deep lake. One day as he leaned over the water to take a drink, wicked old Wetehinen reached up from the bottom of the lake and clutched him by the beard.

"Ouch! Ouch!" the farmer cried. "Let me go!"

Wetehinen only held on more tightly.

"Yes, I'll let you go," he said, "but only on this condition: that you give me one of your daughters for wife!"

"Give you one of my daughters? Never!"

"Very well, then I'll never let go!" wicked old Wetehinen declared and with that he began jerking at the beard as if it were a bellrope.

"Wait! Wait!" the farmer spluttered.

Now he didn't want to give one of his daughters to wicked old Wetehinen—of course not! But at the same time he was in Wetehinen's power and he realized that if he didn't do what the old reprobate demanded he might lose his life and so leave all three of his daughters orphans. Perhaps for the good of all he had better sacrifice one of them.

"All right," he said, "let me go and I'll send you my oldest daughter. I promise."

So Wetehinen let go his beard and the farmer scrambled to his feet and hurried home.

"My dear," he said to his oldest daughter, "I left a bit of the harness down at the lake. Like a good girl will you run down and get it for me."

The eldest daughter went at once and when she reached the water's edge, old Wetehinen reached up and caught her about the waist and carried her down to the bottom of the lake where he lived in a big house.

At first he was kind to her. He made her mistress of the house and gave her the keys to all the rooms and closets. He went very carefully over the keys and pointing to one he said:

"That key you must never use for it opens the door to a room which I forbid you to enter."

The eldest daughter began keeping house for old Wetehinen and spent her time cooking and cleaning and spinning much as she used to at home with her father. The days went by and she grew familiar with the house and began to know what was in every room and every closet.

At first she felt no temptation to open the forbidden door. If old Wetehinen wanted to have a secret room, well and good. But why in the world had he given her the key if he really didn't want her to open the door? The more she thought about it the more she wondered. Every time she passed the room she stopped a moment and stared at the door. It looked just exactly like the doors that led into all the other rooms.

"I wonder why he doesn't want me to open just that door?" she kept asking herself.

Finally one day when old Wetehinen was away she thought:

"I don't believe it would matter if I opened that door just a little crack and peeped in once! No one would know the difference!"

For a few moments she hesitated, then mustered up courage enough to turn the key in the forbidden lock and throw open the door.

The room was a storeroom with boxes and chests and old jars piled up around the wall. That was unexciting enough, but in the middle of the floor was something that made her start when she saw what it was.

It was blood—that's what it was, a pool of dark red blood! She was about to slam the door shut when she saw something else that made her pause. This was a lovely shining ring that lay in the midst of the pool.

"Oh!" she thought to herself, "what a beautiful ring! If I had it I'd wear it on my finger!"

The longer she looked at it, the more she wanted it.

"If I'm very careful," she said, "I know I could reach over and pick it up without touching the blood."

She tiptoed cautiously into the room, wrapped her skirts tightly about her legs, knelt down on the floor, and stretched her arm over the pool. She picked up the ring very carefully but even so she got a few drops of blood on her fingers.

"No matter!" she thought, "I can wash that off! And see the lovely ring!"

But later, after she had the door again locked, when she tried to wash the blood off, she found she couldn't. She tried soap, she tried sand, she tried everything she could think of, but without success.

"I don't care!" she thought to herself. "If Wetehinen sees the blood, I'll just tell him I cut my finger by accident."

So when Wetehinen came home, she hid the ring and pretended nothing was the matter.

After supper Wetehinen put his head in her lap and said:

"Now, my dear, scratch my head and make me drowsy for bed."

She began scratching his head as she had many nights before but, at the first touch of her fingers, he cried out:

"Stop! You're burning my ear! There must be some blood on your fingers! Let me see!"

He reached up and caught her hand and, when he saw the blood stains, he flew into a towering rage.

"I thought so! You've been in the forbidden room!"

He jumped up and without allowing her time to say a word he just cut off her head then and there with no more concern than if she had been a mosquito! After that he took the body and the severed head and threw them into the forbidden room and locked the door.

"Now then," he growled, *"she* won't disobey me again!"

This was all very well but now he had no one to keep house for him and cook and scratch his head in the evening and soon he decided he'd have to get another wife. He remembered that the farmer had two more daughters, so he thought to himself that now he'd marry the second sister.

He waited his chance and one day when the farmer was out in his boat fishing, old Wetehinen came up from the bottom of the lake and clutched the boat. When the poor old farmer tried to row back to shore he couldn't make the boat move an inch. He worked and worked at the oars and wicked old Wetehinen let him struggle until he was exhausted. Then he put his head up out of the water and over the side of the boat and as though nothing were the matter he said:

"Hullo!"

"Oh!" the farmer cried, wishing he were safe on shore, "it's you, is it? I wondered what was holding my boat."

"Yes," wicked old Wetehinen said, "it's me and I'm going to hold your boat right here on this spot until you promise to give me another of your daughters."

What could the farmer do? He pleaded with Wetehinen but Wetehinen was firm and the upshot was that before the farmer again walked dry land he had promised Wetehinen his second daughter.

Well, when he got home, he pretended he had forgotten his ax in the boat and sent his second daughter down to the lake to get it. Wicked old Wetehinen caught her as he had caught her sister and carried her home with him to his house at the bottom of the lake.

Wetehinen treated the second sister just exactly as he had the first, making her mistress of the house and telling her she might use every key but one. Like her sister she, too, after a time gave way to the temptation of looking into the forbidden room and when she saw the shining ring lying in the pool of blood of course she wanted it and of course when she reached to get it she dabbled her fingers in the blood. So that was the end of her, too, for wicked old Wetehinen when he saw the blood stains just cut her head right off and threw her body and the severed head into the forbidden room beside the body and head of her sister and locked the door.

Time went by and the farmer was living happily with his youngest daughter when one day while he was out chopping wood he found a pair of fine birch bark brogues. He put them on and instantly found himself walking away from the woods and down to the lake. He tried to stop but he couldn't. He tried to walk in another direction but the brogues carried him straight down to the water's edge and out into the lake until he was in waist deep.

Then he heard a gruff voice saying:

"Hullo, there! What are you doing with my brogues?"

Of course it was wicked old Wetehinen who had played that trick to get the farmer into his power again.

"What do you want this time?" the poor farmer cried.

"I want your youngest daughter," Wetehinen said.

"What! My youngest daughter!"

"Yes."

"I won't give her up!" the farmer declared. "I don't care what you do to me. I won't give her up!"

"Oh, very well!" Wetehinen said, and immediately the brogues which had been standing still while they talked started walking again. They carried the farmer out into the lake farther and farther until the water was up to his chin.

"Wait—wait a minute!" he cried.

The brogues stopped walking and Wetehinen said:

"Well, do you promise to give her to me?"

"No!" the farmer began. "She's my last daughter and—"

Before he could say more, the brogues walked on and the water rose to his nose. In desperation he threw up his hands and shouted:

"I promise! I promise!"

She fitted the key in the lock

So when he got home that day he said to his youngest daughter whose name was Lisa:

"Lisa, my dear, I forgot my brogues at the lake. Like a good girl won't you run and get them for me?"

So Lisa went to the lake and Wetehinen of course caught her and carried her down to his house as he had her two sisters.

Then the same old story was repeated. Wetehinen made Lisa mistress of the house and gave her keys to all the doors and closets with the same prohibition against opening the door of the forbidden room.

"If I am mistress of the house," Lisa said to herself, "why should I not unlock every door?"

She waited until one day when Wetehinen was away from home, then went boldly to the forbidden room, fitted the key in the lock, and flung open the door.

There lay her two poor sisters with their heads cut off. There in the pool of blood sparkled the lovely ring, but Lisa paid no heed to it.

"Wicked old Wetehinen!" Lisa cried. "I suppose he thinks that ring will tempt me but nothing will tempt me to touch that awful blood!"

Then she rummaged about, opening boxes and chests, and turning things over. In a dark corner she found two pitchers, one marked *Water of Life,* the other *Water of Death.*

"Ha! This is what I want!" she cried, taking the pitcher of the *Water of Life.*

She set the severed heads of her sisters in place and then with the magic water brought them back to life. She used up all the *Water of Life,* so she filled the pitcher marked *Water of Life* with the water from the other pitcher, the *Water of Death.* She hid her sisters each in a big wooden chest, she shut and locked the door of the forbidden room, and Wetehinen when he came home found her working at her spinning wheel as though nothing unusual had happened.

After supper Wetehinen said:

"Now scratch my head and make me drowsy for bed."

So Lisa scratched his wicked old head and she did it so well that he grunted with satisfaction.

"Uh! Uh!" he said. "That's good! Now just behind my right ear! That's it! That's it! You're a good girl, you are! You're not like some of them who do what they're told not to do! Now behind the other ear! Oh, that's fine! Yes, you're a good girl and if there's anything you want me to do just tell me what it is."

"I want to send a chest of things to my poor old father," Lisa said. "Just a lot of little nothings—odds and ends that I've picked up about the house. I'd be ashamed to have you open the chest and see them. I do wish you'd carry the chest ashore to-morrow and leave it where my father will find it."

"All right, I will," Wetehinen promised.

He was true to his word. The next morning he hoisted one of the chests on his shoulder, the one that had in it the eldest sister, he trudged off with it, and tossed it up on shore at a place where he was sure the farmer would find it.

Lisa then wheedled him into carrying up the second chest that had in it the second sister. This time Wetehinen wasn't so good-natured.

"I don't know what she can always be sending her father!" he grumbled. "If she sends another chest I'll have to look inside and see."

Now Lisa, when the second sister was safely delivered, began to plan her own escape. She pulled out another empty chest and then one evening after she had succeeded in making old Wetehinen comfortable and drowsy she begged him to carry this also to her father. He grumbled and protested but finally promised.

"And you won't look inside, will you? Promise me you won't!" Lisa begged.

Wetehinen said he wouldn't, but he intended to just the same.

Well, the next morning as soon as Wetehinen went out, Lisa took the churn and dressed it up in some of her own clothes. She carried it to the top of the house and perched it on the ridge of the roof before a spinning wheel. Then she herself crept inside the third chest and waited.

When Wetehinen came home he looked up and saw what he thought was Lisa spinning on the roof.

"Hullo!" he shouted. "What are you doing up there?"

Lisa, in the chest, answered in a voice that sounded as if it came from the roof:

"I'm spinning. And you, Wetehinen, my dear, don't forget the chest that you promised to carry to my poor old father. It's standing in the kitchen."

Wetehinen grumbled but because of his promise he hoisted the chest on his shoulder and started off. When he had gone a little way he thought to put it down and take a peep inside. Instantly Lisa's voice, sounding as if it came from the roof, cried out:

"No! No! You promised not to look inside!"

"I'm not looking inside!" Wetehinen called back. "I'm only resting a minute!"

Then he thought to himself:

"I suppose she's sitting up there so she can watch me!"

When he had gone some distance farther, he thought again to set down the chest and open the lid but instantly Lisa's voice, as from a long way off, called out:

"No! No! You promised not to look inside!"

"Who's looking inside?" he called back, pretending again he was only resting.

Every time he thought it would be safe to put down the chest and open the lid, Lisa's voice cried out:

"No! No! You promised not to!"

"Mercy on us!" old Wetehinen fumed to himself, "who would have thought she could see so far!"

On the shore of the lake when he threw down the chest in disgust he tried one last time to raise the lid. Instantly Lisa's voice cried out:

"No! No! You promised not to!"

"I'm not looking inside!" Wetehinen roared, and in a fury he left the chest and started back into the water.

All the way home he grumbled and growled:

"A nice way to treat a man, always making him

carry chests! I won't carry another one no matter how much she begs me!"

When he came near home he saw the spinning wheel still on the roof and the figure still seated before it.

"Why haven't you got my dinner ready?" he called out angrily.

The figure at the spinning wheel made no answer.

"What's the matter with you?" Wetehinen cried. "Why are you sitting there like a wooden image instead of cooking my dinner?"

Still the figure made no answer and in a rage Wetehinen began climbing up the roof. He reached out blindly and clutched at Lisa's skirt and jerked it so hard that the churn came clattering down on his head. It knocked him off the roof and he fell all the way to the ground and cracked his wicked old head wide open.

"Ouch! Ouch!" he roared in pain. "Just wait till I get hold of that Lisa!"

He crawled to the forbidden room and poured over himself the water that was in the pitcher marked *Water of Life*. But it wasn't the *Water of Life* at all, it was the *Water of Death*, and so it didn't help his wicked old cracked head at all. In fact it just made it worse and worse *and* worse.

THE THREE CHESTS 65

Lisa and her sisters were never again troubled by him nor was any one else that lived on the shores of that lake.

"Wonder what's become of wicked old Wetehinen?" people began saying.

Lisa thought she knew but she didn't tell.

LOG

The Story of the Hero Who Released the Sun

LOG

There was once a poor couple who had no children. Their neighbors all had boys and girls in plenty but for some reason God didn't send them even one.

"If I can't have a flesh and blood baby," the woman said one day, "I'm going to have a wooden baby."

She went to the woods and cut a log of alder just the size of a nice fat baby. She dressed the log in baby clothes and put it in a cradle. Then for three whole years she and her husband rocked the cradle and sang lullabies to the log baby.

At the end of three years one afternoon, when the man was out chopping wood and the woman was driving the cows home from pasture, the log baby turned into a real baby! It was so strong and hearty that by the time its parents got home it had crawled out of the cradle and was sitting on the floor yelling lustily for food. It ate and ate and ate and the more it ate the faster it grew. It wasn't any time at all in passing from babyhood to childhood, from childhood to youth, and from youth to manhood. From its beginnings it was known in the village as Log and never received any other name.

Log's parents knew from the first that Log was destined to be a great hero. That was why he was so strong and so good. There was no one in the village as strong as he nor any one as kind and gentle.

Now just at this time a great calamity overtook the world. The Sun and the Moon and the Dawn disappeared from the sky and as a result the earth was left in darkness.

"Who have taken from us the Sun and the Moon and the Dawn?" the people cried in terror.

"Whoever they are," the King said, "they shall have to restore them! Where, O where are the heroes who will undertake to find the Sun and the Moon and the Dawn and return them to their places in the sky?"

There were many men willing to offer themselves for the great adventure but the King realized that something more was needed than willingness.

"It is only heroes of exceptional strength and endurance," he said, "who should risk the dangers of so perilous an undertaking."

So he called together all the valiant youths of the kingdom and tested them one by one. He had some waters of great strength and it was his hope to find three heroes the first of whom could drink three bottles of the strong waters, the second six bottles, and the third nine bottles.

Hundreds of youths presented themselves and out of them all the King found at last two, one of whom was able to take three bottles of the strong waters, the other six bottles.

"But we need three heroes!" the King cried. "Is there no one in all this kingdom strong enough to drink nine bottles?"

"Try Log!" some one shouted.

All the youths present instantly took up the cry:

"Log! Log! Send for Log!"

So the King sent for Log and sure enough when Log came he was able to drink down nine bottles of the strong waters without any trouble at all.

"Here now," the King proclaimed, "are the three heroes who are to release the Sun and the Moon and the Dawn from whoever are holding them in captivity and restore them to their places in the sky!"

He equipped the three heroes for a long journey furnishing them money and food and drink of the strong waters, each according to his strength. He mounted them each on a mighty horse with sword and arrow and dog.

So the three heroes rode off in the dark and the women of the kingdom wept to see them go and the men cheered and wished that they, too, were going.

They rode on and on for many days that seemed like nights until they had crossed the confines of their own country and entered the boundaries of an unknown kingdom beyond. Here the darkness was less dense. There was no actual daylight but a faint grayness as of approaching dawn.

They rode on until they saw looming up before them the towers of a mighty castle. They dismounted near the castle at the door of a little hut where they found an old woman.

"Good day to you, granny!" Log called out.

"Good day, indeed!" the old woman said. "It's little enough we see of the day since the Evil One cursed the Sun and handed it over to Suyettar's wicked offspring, the Nine-Headed Serpent!"

"The Evil One!" Log exclaimed. "Tell me, granny, why did the Evil One curse the Sun?"

"Because he's evil, my son, that's why! He said the Sun's rays blistered him, so he cursed the Sun and gave him over to the Nine-Headed Serpent. And he cursed the Moon, too, because at night when the Moon shone he could not steal. Yes, my son, he cursed the Moon and handed her over to Suyettar's second offspring, the Six-Headed Serpent. Then he cursed the Dawn because he said he couldn't sleep in the morning because of the Dawn. So he cursed the Dawn and gave her over to Suyettar's third offspring, the Three-Headed Serpent."

"Tell me, granny," Log said, "where do the three Serpents keep prisoner the Sun and the Moon and the Dawn?"

"Listen, my son, and I will tell you: When they go far out in the Ocean they carry with them the Sun and the Moon and the Dawn. The Three-Headed Serpent stays out there one day and then returns at night. The Six-Headed Serpent stays two days and then returns, and the mighty Nine-Headed Monster does not return until the third night. As each returns a faint glow spreads over the land. That is why we are not in utter darkness."

Log thanked the old woman and then he and his companions pushed on towards the castle. As they neared it they saw a strange sight which they could not understand. One half of the great castle was laughing and rocking as if in merriment and the other half was weeping as if in grief.

"What can this mean?" Log cried out. "We had better ask the old woman before we go on."

So they went back to the hut and the old woman told them all she knew.

"It is on account of the dreadful fate that is hanging over the King's three daughters," she said. "Those three evil Monsters are demanding them one by one. To-night when the Three-Headed Serpent comes back from the Ocean he expects to devour the eldest. If the King refuses to give her up, then Suyettar's evil son will devour half the kingdom, half of the castle itself, and half the shining stones. O that some hero would kill the monster and save the princess and at the same time release the Dawn that it might again steal over the world!"

Log and his fellows conferred together and the one they called Three Bottles, because his strength was equal to three bottles of the strong waters, declared that it was his task to fight and conquer the Three-Headed Serpent.

In the castle meanwhile preparations for the sacrifice of the oldest princess were going forward. As the King sewed the poor girl into a great leather sack, his tears fell so fast that he could scarcely see what he was doing.

"My dear child," he said, "it should comfort you greatly to think that the Monster is going to eat you instead of half the kingdom! Not many princesses are considered as important as half the kingdom!"

The princess knew that what her father said must be true and she did her best to look cheerful as they slipped the sack over her head. Once inside, however, she allowed herself to cry for she knew that no one could see her.

The sack with the princess inside was carried down to the beach and put on a high rock near the place where Suyettar's sons were wont to come up out of the water.

"Don't be frightened, my daughter!" the King called out as he and all the Court started back to the castle. "You won't have long to wait, for it will soon be evening."

Log and his companions watched the King's party disappear and then Three Bottles solemnly drank down the three bottles of strong waters with which his own King had equipped him. As he was ready to mount his horse, he handed Log the leash to which his dog was attached.

"If I need help," he said, "I'll throw back my shoe and do you then release my dog."

With that he rode boldly down to the beach, dismounted, and climbed up the rock where the unfortunate princess lay in a sack. With one slash of the sword he ripped open the sack and dragged the princess out. She supposed of course that he was the Three-Headed Serpent and at first was so frightened that she kept her eyes tightly shut not daring to look at him. She expected every minute to have him take a first bite and, when minutes and more minutes and more minutes still went by and he didn't, she opened her eyes a little crack to see what was the matter.

"Oh!" the princess said.

She was so surprised that for a long time she didn't dare to take another peep.

"You thought I was the Three-Headed Serpent, didn't you?" a pleasant voice asked. "But I'm not. I'm only a young man who has come to rescue you."

The princess murmured, "Oh!" again, but this time the "Oh!" expressed happy relief.

"Yes," repeated the young man, "I am the hero who has come to rescue you. My comrades call me Three Bottles and you, too, may call me that. And while we are waiting for the Serpent to come in from the Ocean I wish you would scratch my head."

The princess wasn't in the least surprised at this request. Heroes and monsters and fathers alike seemed always to want their heads scratched.

So Three Bottles stretched himself at the princess' feet and put his head in her lap. He settled himself comfortably and she scratched his head while he gazed out over the dark Ocean waiting for the Serpent to appear.

At first there was nothing to break the glassy surface of the water. They waited and at last far out they saw three swirling masses rolling landward.

"Quick, my princess!" Three Bottles cried. "There comes the Monster now! Get you down behind the rock and hide there while I go meet the creature and chop off his ugly heads!"

The princess, quivering with fright, crouched down behind the rock and Three Bottles, mounting his horse, rode boldly down to the water's edge awaiting the Serpent's coming.

It came nearer and nearer in long easy swirls, slowly lifting its three scaly heads one after another.

As it approached shore it sniffed the air hungrily.

"Fee, fi, fo, fum!" it muttered in a deep voice,

repeating the magic rime it had learned from its evil mother, Suyettar:

> "Fee, fi, fo, fum!
> I smell a Finn! Yum! Yum!
> I'll fall upon him with a thud!
> I'll pick his bones and drink his blood!
> Fee, fi, fo, fum!
> Yum! Yum!"

"Stop boasting, son of Suyettar!" Three Bottles cried. "You'll have time enough to boast after you fight!"

"Fight?" repeated the Serpent as if in surprise. "Shall we fight, pretty boy, you and I? Very well! Blow then with your sweet breath, blow out a long level platform of red copper whereon we can meet and try our strength each with the other!"

"Nay," answered Three Bottles. "Do you blow with your evil breath and instead of red copper we shall have a platform of black iron."

So the Serpent blew and on the iron platform that came of his breath Three Bottles met him in combat. Back and forth they raged, Three Bottles striking right and left with his mighty sword, the Serpent hitting at Three Bottles with all his scaly heads and belching forth fire and smoke from all his mouths. Three Bottles whacked off one scaly head and at last a second one, but he was unable to touch the third.

"I shall have to have help," he acknowledged to himself finally, and reaching down he took one of his shoes and threw it over his shoulder back to his comrades who were awaiting the outcome of the struggle. Instantly they loosed the dog which bounded forward to its master's assistance and soon with the dog's help Three Bottles was able to dispatch the last head.

He was faint now with weariness and his comrades had to help him back to the old woman's hut where he soon fell asleep.

Night passed and Dawn appeared. A great cry of relief and thanksgiving went up from all the earth.

"The Dawn! The Dawn!" people cried. "God bless the man who has released the Dawn!"

Only at the castle was there sorrow still.

"My poor oldest daughter!" the King cried with tears in his eyes. "It was my sacrifice of her that has released the Dawn!"

Then he called his slaves and gave them orders to gather up his daughter's bones and to bring back the leather sack.

"We shall need it again to-night," he said. He wiped

his eyes and for a moment could say no more. "Yes, to-night we shall have to sew up my second daughter and offer her to the Six-Headed Serpent, him that holds captive the Moon. Otherwise the monster will devour half my kingdom, half the castle, and half the shining stones. Ai! Ai! Ai!"

But the slaves when they went to the high rock on the seashore found, not the princess' bones, but the princess herself, sitting there with her chin in her hand, gazing down on the beach which was strewn with the fragments of the Three-Headed Serpent.

They led her back to her father and reported the marvel they had seen.

"There, O King, lies the monster on the sand with all his heads severed! So huge are the heads that it would need three men with derricks to move one of them!"

"Some unknown hero has rescued my oldest daughter!" the King cried. "Would that another might come to-night to rescue my second child likewise! But, alas! what hero is strong enough to destroy the Six-Headed Monster!"

So when evening came they sewed the second princess in the sack and carried her out to the rock.

Log and his companions saw the procession move down from the castle and they saw that the castle was again disturbed, one half of it laughing and one half weeping.

"It's the second princess to-night," the old woman told them. "Unless her father, the King, gives her to the Six-Headed Serpent, the Monster will come and devour half the kingdom, half the castle, and half the shining stones. He it is that holds the Moon captive and the hero that slays him will release the Moon."

Then he whom his comrades called Six Bottles cried out:

"Here is work for me!"

He drank bottle after bottle of the strong waters until he had emptied six.

"Now I am ready!" he shouted.

He mounted his mighty horse and as he rode off he called to his comrades:

"If I need help I'll throw back a shoe and do you then unleash my dog!"

He rode to the rock on the shore and dismounted. Then he climbed the rock and released the second princess. He told her who he was and as they awaited the arrival of the Six-Headed Serpent he lay at the princess' feet and she scratched his head.

This time the Serpent came in six mighty swirls with six awful heads that reared up one after another.

In terror the second princess hid behind the rock while Six Bottles, mounting his horse, rode boldly down to the water's edge.

Like his brother Serpent this one, too, came sniffing the air hungrily, muttering the magic rime he had learned from his mother, wicked Suyettar:

> "Fee, fi, fo, fum!
> I smell a Finn! Yum! Yum!
> I'll fall upon him with a thud!
> I'll pick his bones and drink his blood!
> Fee, fi, fo, fum!
> Yum! Yum!"

"Stop boasting, son of an evil mother!" Six Bottles cried. "You will have time enough to boast after you fight!"

"Fight?" repeated the Serpent scornfully. "Shall we fight, little one, you and I? Very well! Blow then with your sweet breath, blow out a long level platform of white silver whereon we can meet and try our strength one with the other."

"Nay!" answered Six Bottles. "Do you blow, blow with your evil breath, and instead of white silver we shall have a platform of red copper."

So the Serpent blew and on the copper platform that

came of his breath Six Bottles met him in combat. Back and forth they raged, Six Bottles striking left and right with his mighty sword, the Serpent hitting at Six Bottles with every one of his six scaly heads and belching forth fire and smoke from all his mouths. Six Bottles whacked off one head, then another, then another. At last he had disposed of five heads. He tried hard to strike the last, but by this time the Serpent had grown wary and Six Bottles' own strength was waning. So he reached down and took one of his shoes and threw it over his shoulder back to his comrades who were awaiting the outcome of the struggle. Instantly they loosed the dog which bounded forward to its master's assistance and soon with the dog's help Six Bottles was able to dispatch the last head.

Then his comrades led him, weary from the fight, to the old woman's hut and soon he fell asleep.

While he slept the Moon appeared in the sky and a great cry of relief and thanksgiving went up from all the world:

"The Moon! The Moon! God bless the man who has released the Moon!"

The King who was awakened by the sound looked out the castle window and when he saw the Moon, returned to its place in the sky, his eyes overflowed with grief.

"My poor second daughter!" he cried. "It was my sacrifice of her that has released the Moon! To-morrow morning I will send the slaves to gather up her bones and to bring back the leather sack into which, alas! I must then sew my youngest daughter for evil Suyettar's third son, the Nine-Headed Serpent. Ai! Ai! Ai! How sad it is to be a father!"

But on the morrow when the slaves went to the rock they found the second princess sitting there alone gazing down upon the scattered fragments of the Six-Headed Serpent.

"Here she is, safe and sound!" they reported to the King as they led the second princess into his presence, "and, marvel of marvels! on the beach below the rock lies the body of the Six-Headed Serpent torn to pieces! Its heads, O King, are so monstrous that six men with derricks could scarcely move one of them!"

"God be praised!" the King cried. "Another unknown hero has come and saved the life of my second child! Would that a third might come to-night and rescue the life of my youngest child! Alas, she is dearer to me than both the others, but I fear me that even if there be heroes who could dispatch the first two Serpents, there is never one who can touch him of the Nine Heads that holds the mighty Sun a captive!"

"This last and mightiest battle is for me!"

And the poor King wept, so sure was he that nothing could save the life of his youngest child.

When Log and his companions heard of the King's grief, Log at once stood forth and said:

"This last and mightiest battle is for me!"

He opened the strong waters and drank bottle after bottle until he had emptied nine.

"Now let night come as soon as it will!" he cried. "I am ready for the Monster!"

He started forth telling his comrades he would throw back a shoe if he needed help from his dog.

So it was Log himself who slashed open the sack for the third time and released the Youngest Princess who was much more beautiful than her sisters. She fell in love with the mighty hero on sight and was so thrilled with his godlike beauty that when he put his head in her lap she hardly knew what to do although her father always declared that she scratched his head much better than either of her sisters.

They had not long to wait for soon all the Ocean was a glitter with the swirls of the ninefold Monster who was coming to shore with the captive Sun in his keeping.

"Await me behind the rock!" Log cried to the Princess as he leapt upon his horse and started forward.

"Oh, Log, my hero, be careful!" the Princess cried after him.

Nearer and nearer came the swirls of the nine-coiled Monster. One after another of his nine heads rose and fell as he approached, and every head sniffed more hungrily as it came nearer, and each head rumbled as it sniffed:

> "Fee, fi, fo, fum!
> I smell a Finn! Yum! Yum!
> I'll fall upon him with a thud!
> I'll pick his bones and drink his blood!
> Fee, fi, fo, fum!
> Yum! Yum!"

"Stop boasting, evil son of an evil mother!" Log cried. "You will have time enough to boast after you fight!"

"Fight?" roared the awful Monster. "Shall we fight, poor infant, you and I? Very well! Blow then with your sweet breath, blow out a long level platform of shining gold whereon we can meet and try our strength each with the other!"

"Nay!" Log answered boldly. "Do you blow, blow with your evil breath and instead of shining gold we shall have a platform of white silver."

So the Monster blew and on the silver platform that came of his breath Log met him in combat. Back and forth they raged, Log striking right and left with his mighty sword, the Serpent hitting at Log with all his nine scaly heads and belching forth fire and smoke from all his nine mouths. Log whacked off head after head until six lay gaping on the sand. But the last three he could not get.

Suddenly he pointed behind the Serpent and cried: "Quick! Quick! The Sun! It is escaping!"

The Serpent looked around and Log whacked off a head. Now only two remained, but try as he would Log could get neither of them.

Again he tried a subterfuge.

"Your wife, O Son of Suyettar! See, yonder, they're abusing her!"

The Monster looked and Log whacked off another head. But one now remained and as usual it was the hardest of them all to get. Log felt his strength waning while the Monster seemed more nimble than ever.

"I shall have to have help," Log thought.

He threw back his shoe to his comrades and they at once loosed his dog. With the dog's help Log was soon able to dispatch the last head. Then Three Bottles and Six Bottles helped him off his horse and supported him to the old woman's hut where he soon fell into a deep sleep.

The next morning the blessed Sun rose at his proper time and people all over the world, falling on their knees with thanksgiving and weeping with joy, cried out:

"The Sun! The Sun! God bless the man who has released the Sun!"

At the castle they waked the King with the good news but the King only shook his head and murmured in grief:

"Yes, the Sun is released but what care I since my favorite child, my youngest daughter, has been sacrificed!"

He dispatched the slaves to gather up her bones and presently these returned bringing the Princess herself and telling a marvelous tale of the beach littered with nine severed heads so huge that it would need nine men with derricks to move one of them.

"What manner of heroes are these who have rescued my daughters!" cried the King. "Let them come forth and I will give them my daughters for wives and half my riches for dowry! But they will have to prove themselves the actual heroes by bringing to the castle the heavy heads of the Monsters they have slain."

When Log and his fellows heard this they laughed

with happiness and, strengthening themselves with deep draughts of the strong waters, they gathered together the many heads of the mighty Serpents, bore them to the castle, and piled them up at the King's feet.

Then Log stepped forward and said:

"Here we are, O King, come to claim our reward!"

The King, true to his promise, gave them his daughters in marriage, the oldest to Three Bottles, the second to Six Bottles, and the lovely Youngest to Log. Then he apportioned them the half of his riches and, after much feasting and merrymaking, the heroes took their brides and their riches and bidding the King farewell started homewards.

As they rode through a great forest they sighted a tiny hut and Log, motioning his comrades to wait for him quietly, crept forward to see who was in the hut. It was well he was cautious for inside the hut was Suyettar herself talking to two other old hags.

"Ay," she was saying, "they have slain my three beautiful sons, my mighty offspring that held captive the Sun and the Moon and the Dawn! But I tell you, sisters, they will pay the penalty. . . ."

To hear better Log changed himself into a piece of firewood and slipping inside the hut hid himself in the woodpile near the stove.

"Ay, they will pay the penalty!" Suyettar repeated. "I shall have my revenge on them! A fine supper Suyettar shall soon have, yum, yum!

> I'll fall upon them with a thud!
> I'll pick their bones and drink their blood!

Fools, fools, to think they can escape Suyettar's anger!"

"But sister, sister," the two old hags asked, "how will you get them?"

Suyettar looked this way and that to make sure that no one was listening. Then she whispered:

"This is how I shall get them: As they come through this forest, the three men with their brides, I shall send upon them a terrible hunger. Then they shall come suddenly upon a table spread with tempting food. One bite of that food and they are in my power, he-he! Ay, sisters, to-night Suyettar will have a fine supper! Nothing can save them unless, before they touch the food, some one make the sign of the cross three times over the table. Then table and food would disappear and also the ravening hunger. But even if that happens Suyettar shall still get them!"

"How, sister, how?" the other two asked.

"Presently I should send upon them consuming thirst, and then put in their pathway a spring of cold sparkling water. One drop of that water and they are in my power, he-he! Nothing can save them from me unless, before their lips touch the water, some one make the sign of the cross three times over the spring. At that the spring would disappear and also their thirst. But even if they escape the spring, I shall still get them. I shall send great heaviness on them and a longing for sleep, then let them come upon a row of soft inviting feather beds. If they cast themselves upon the beds, they are mine, he-he! to feast upon as I will! Nothing can save but that some one make the sign of the cross three times over the beds before they touch them. Oh, sisters, I shall get them one way or another for there is no one to warn them. If there was any one to warn them, he wouldn't dare tell them what he knows for he would also know that if he told them he would himself be turned into a blue cross and have to stand forever in the cemetery."

As Log knew now all the dangers that threatened, he slipped away from the woodpile and, when he was outside, took his own shape and hurried back to his comrades.

"Away!" he cried. "We are in great danger!"

They all spurred their horses and rode swiftly on until Three Bottles suddenly cried:

"Hold, comrades, hold! I am faint with hunger!"

"Me, too!" cried Six Bottles.

At that instant a great table, laden with delicious food, appeared before them.

"Look!" cried the one of them.

"Food!" cried the other.

They flung themselves from their horses and ran towards the table. But quick as they were, Log was quicker. He reached the table first and, raising his hand, made the sign of the cross three times. The table disappeared as suddenly as it had come and with it the strange hunger that had but now consumed them.

"Strange!" Three Bottles exclaimed. "I thought I was hungry, but I'm not!"

"I thought I saw food just now," Six Bottles said. "I must have been dreaming."

So they mounted again and pushed on.

"Danger threatens us," said Log. "We must hurry and not dismount no matter what the temptation."

They agreed but presently one of them cried out and then the other:

"Water! Water! We shall soon perish unless we have water!"

Instantly by the wayside appeared a spring of cool sparkling water and it was all Log could do to reach it before his fellows. He did get there first and make the sign of the cross three times whereat the spring disappeared and with it the thirst which had but now consumed them all.

"I thought I was thirsty," Three Bottles said, "but I'm not!"

"Why did we dismount?" Six Bottles asked. "There's no water here."

So again they mounted and went forward and Log, warning them again that danger threatened, begged them not to dismount a third time no matter what the temptation.

They promised they would not but presently, complaining of fatigue, they wanted to. Their brides, too, swayed in the saddle, overcome with weariness and sleep.

"Dear Log," they said, "let us rest for an hour. See, our brides are drooping with fatigue! One hour's sleep and we shall all be refreshed!"

Instantly beside them on the forest floor they saw three soft white feather beds. Log leaped to the ground but before he was able to make the sign of the cross over more than one of the beds, his comrades and their brides had fallen headlong on the other two.

And that was the end of poor Three Bottles and Six Bottles and their two lovely brides. There was no way now of saving them from Suyettar. She had them in her power and nothing would induce her to give them up.

As Log and his bride sadly mounted their horse and rode on they heard an evil voice chanting out in triumph:

> "I'll fall upon them with a thud, he-he!
> I'll pick their bones and drink their blood, he-he!"

"Poor fellows! Poor fellows!" Log said, and the Princess wept to think of the awful fate that had overtaken her two sisters.

Well, Log and his bride reached home without further adventure and were received by the King with great honors.

"I knew my heroes were succeeding," the King said, "when first the Dawn appeared again, and then the Moon, and last the mighty Sun. All hail to you, Log, and to your two comrades! But, by the way, where are Three Bottles and Six Bottles?"

"Your Majesty," Log said, "Three Bottles and Six Bottles were brave men both. By their prowess they released the one the Dawn, the other the Moon. Then in an evil adventure on the way home they perished. I can tell you no more."

"You can tell me no more?" the King said. "Why

can you tell me no more? What was the evil adventure in which they perished?"

"If I told you, O King, then I, too, should perish, for I should be turned into a blue cross and stood forever in the cemetery!"

"What nonsense!" the King exclaimed. "Who would turn you into a blue cross and stand you forever in the cemetery?"

"That is what I cannot tell you," Log said.

The King laughed and pressed Log no further, but the people of the kingdom, scenting a mystery, insisted on knowing in detail what had happened the other two heroes. Presently the rumor began to spread that Log himself had done away with them in order that he might gather to himself all the glory of the undertaking.

The King was forced at last to send for him again and to demand a full account of everything.

Log realized that his end was near. He met it bravely. Commending to the King's protection his lovely bride, the Youngest Princess, Log related how the three mighty Serpents whom they had killed were sons of Suyettar, and how in revenge Suyettar had succeeded in destroying Three Bottles and Six Bottles together with their brides. Then he told the fate about to overtake himself.

He finished speaking and as the King and the Court looked at him, to their amazement he disappeared.

"To the cemetery!" some one cried.

They all went to the cemetery where at once they found a fresh blue cross that had come there nobody knew how. There it stands to this day, a reminder of the life and deeds of the mighty hero, Log.

The King was overcome with sorrow at losing such a hero. He took Log's bride under his protection and he found her so beautiful and so gentle that soon he fell in love with her and married her.

THE LITTLE SISTER

The Story of Suyettar and the Nine Brothers

THE LITTLE SISTER

 There was once a woman who had nine sons. They were good boys and loved her dearly but there was one thing about which they were always complaining.

"Why haven't we a little sister?" they kept asking. "Do give us a little sister!"

When the time came that another child was to be born, they said to their mother:

"If the baby is a boy we are going away and you will never see us again, but if it is a little girl then we shall stay home and take care of it."

The mother agreed that if the child were a girl she would have her husband put a spindle outside on the gatepost and, if it were a boy, an ax.

"Just wait," she said, "and see what your father puts on the gatepost and then you will know whether it is another brother God has sent you or a little sister."

The baby turned out to be a girl and the mother was overjoyed.

"Hurry, husband!" she cried, "and put a spindle on the gatepost so that our nine sons may know the good news!"

The man did so and then quickly returned to the mother and baby. The moment he was gone Suyettar slipped up and changed the tokens. She took away the spindle and put in its place an ax. Then with an evil grin she hurried off mumbling to herself:

"Now we'll see what we'll see!"

She hoped to bring trouble and grief and she succeeded. As soon as the nine sons saw the ax on the gatepost they thought their mother had given birth to another son and at once they left home vowing never to return.

The poor mother waited for them and waited.

"What is keeping my sons?" she cried at last. "Go out to the gate, husband, and see if they are coming."

The man went out and soon returned bringing back word that some one had changed the tokens.

"The spindle that I put on the gatepost is gone," he said, "and in its place is an ax."

"Alas!" cried the poor mother, "some evil creature has done this to spite us! Oh, if we could only get word to our sons of the little sister they were so eager to have!"

But there was no way to reach them for no one knew the way they had gone.

In a short time the husband died and the poor woman, abandoned by her nine sons, had only her little daughter left. She named the child Kerttu. Kerttu was a dear little girl and her face was as beautiful as her heart was good. Whenever she found her mother weeping alone she tried to comfort her and, as she grew older, she wanted to know the cause of her mother's grief. At last the mother told her about her nine brothers and how they had gone away never to return owing to the trick of some evil creature.

"My poor mother!" she cried, "how sorry I am that I am the innocent cause of your loss! Let me go out into the world and find my brothers! When once they hear the truth they will gladly come home to you to care for you in your old age!"

At first the mother would not consent to this.

"You are all I have," she said, "and I should indeed be miserable and lonely if anything happened you!"

But Kerttu continued to weep every time she thought of her poor brothers driven unnecessarily from home and at last the mother, realizing that she would nevermore be happy unless she were allowed to go in search of them, gave up opposing her.

"Very well, my daughter, you may go and may God go with you and bring you safely back to me. But before you go I must prepare you a bag of food for the journey and bake you a magic cake that will show you the way."

So she baked a batch of bread and at the same time mixed a little round cake with Kerttu's own tears and baked it, too. Then she said:

"Here now, my child, are provisions for the journey and here is a magic cake that will lead you to your brothers. All you have to do is throw it down in front of you and say:

> 'Roll, roll, my little cake!
> Show me the way that I must take
> To find at last the brothers nine
> Whose own true mother is also mine!'

Then the little cake will start rolling and do you follow wherever it rolls. But, Kerttu, my child, you must not start out alone. You must have some friend or companion to go with you."

Now it happened that Kerttu had a little dog, Musti, that she loved dearly.

"I'll take Musti with me!" she said. "Musti will protect me!"

THE LITTLE SISTER 105

So she called Musti and Musti wagged his tail and barked with joy at the prospect of going out into the world with his mistress.

Then Kerttu threw down the magic cake in front of her and sang:

> "Roll, roll, my little cake!
> Show me the way that I must take
> To find at last the brothers nine
> Whose own true mother is also mine!"

At once the cake rolled off like a little wheel and Kerttu and Musti followed it. They walked until they were tired. Then Kerttu picked up the little cake and they rested by the wayside. When they were ready again to start the cake a-rolling, all Kerttu had to do was throw it down in front of her and say the magic rime.

Their first day was without adventure. When night came they ate their supper and went to sleep in a field under a tree.

The second day they overtook an ugly old woman whom Kerttu disliked on sight. But she said to herself:

"Shame on you, Kerttu, not liking this woman just because she's old and ugly!" and she made herself answer the old woman's greetings politely and she made Musti stop snarling and growling.

The old hag asked Kerttu who she was and where she was going and Kerttu told her.

"Ah!" said the old woman, "how fortunate that we have met each other for our ways lie together!"

She smiled and petted Kerttu's arm and Kerttu felt like shuddering. But she restrained herself and told herself severely:

"You're a wicked girl not to feel more friendly to the poor old thing!"

Musti felt much as Kerttu did. He no longer growled for Kerttu had told him not to, but he drooped his tail between his legs and, pressing up close to Kerttu, he trembled with fright. And well he might, too, for the old hag was none other than Suyettar who had been waiting all these years just for this very chance to do further injury to Kerttu and her brothers.

Kerttu, poor child, was, alas! too good and innocent to suspect evil in others. She said to Suyettar:

"Very well, if our ways lie together then we can be companions."

So Suyettar joined Kerttu and Musti and the three of them walked on following the little cake. As the day advanced the sun grew hotter and hotter and at last when they reached a lake Suyettar said:

"My dear, let us sit down here for a few moments and rest."

They all sat down and presently Suyettar said:

"Let us go bathing in the lake. That will refresh us."

Kerttu would have agreed if Musti had not tugged at her skirts and warned her not to.

"Don't do it, dear mistress!" Musti growled softly. "Don't go in bathing with her! She'll bewitch you!"

So Kerttu said:

"No, I don't want to go in bathing."

Suyettar waited until they were again journeying on and then when Kerttu wasn't looking she turned around and kicked Musti and broke one of the poor little dog's legs. Thereafter Musti had to hop along on three legs.

The next afternoon when they passed another lake, Suyettar tried again to tempt Kerttu into the water.

"The sun is very hot," she said, "and it would refresh us both to bathe. Come, Kerttu, my dear, don't refuse me this time!"

But again Musti tugged at Kerttu's skirts and, licking her hand, whispered the warning:

"Don't do it, dear mistress! Don't go in bathing with her or she will bewitch you!"

So again Kerttu said politely:

"No, I don't feel like going in bathing. You go in alone and I'll wait for you here."

But this was not what Suyettar wanted and she said, no, she didn't care to go in alone. She was furious, too, with Musti and later when Kerttu wasn't looking she gave the poor little dog a kick that broke another leg. Thereafter Musti had to hop along on two legs.

They slept the third night by the wayside and the next day they went on again always following the magic cake. In midafternoon they passed a lake and Suyettar said:

"Surely, my dear, you must be tired and hot. Let us both bathe in this cool lake."

But Musti, hopping painfully along on two legs, yelped weakly and said to Kerttu:

"Don't do it, dear mistress! Don't go in bathing with her or she'll bewitch you!"

So for a third time Kerttu refused and later, when she wasn't looking, Suyettar kicked Musti and broke the third of the poor little dog's legs. Thereafter Musti hopped on as best he could on only one leg.

Well, they went on and on. When night came they

slept by the roadside and then next morning they started on again. The sun grew hot and by midafternoon Kerttu was tired and ready to rest. When they reached a lake Suyettar again begged that they both go in bathing. Kerttu was tempted to agree when poor Musti threw himself panting at her feet and whimpered:

"Don't do it, dear mistress! Don't go in bathing with her or she will bewitch you!"

So Kerttu again refused.

"That's right, dear mistress!" Musti panted, "don't do it! I shall soon be dead, I know, for she hates me, but before I die I want to warn you one last time never to go in bathing with her or she will bewitch you!"

"What's that dog saying?" Suyettar demanded angrily, and without waiting for an answer she picked up a heavy piece of wood and struck poor Musti such a blow on the head that it killed him.

"What have you done to my poor little dog?" Kerttu cried.

"Don't mind him, my dear," Suyettar said. "He was sick and lame and it was better to put him out of his misery."

Suyettar tried to soothe Kerttu and make her forget Musti but all afternoon Kerttu wept to think that she would never again see her faithful little friend.

The next afternoon when Suyettar begged her to go in bathing there was no Musti to warn her against it and at last Kerttu allowed herself to be persuaded. She was tired from her many days' wandering and it was true that the first touch of the cool water refreshed her.

"Now splash water in my face!" Suyettar cried.

But Kerttu didn't want to splash water into Suyettar's face for she supposed Suyettar was an old woman and she thought it would be disrespectful to splash water into the face of an old woman.

"Do you hear me!" screamed Suyettar.

When Kerttu still hesitated, Suyettar looked at her with such a terrible, threatening expression that Kerttu did as she was bidden. She splashed water into Suyettar's face and, as the water touched Suyettar's eyes, Suyettar cried out:

> "Your bonny looks give up to me
> And you take mine for all to see!"

Instantly they two changed appearance: Suyettar looked young and beautiful like Kerttu, and Kerttu was changed to a hideous old hag. Then too late she realized that the awful old woman to whom she had been so polite was Suyettar.

Suyettar bewitching Kerttu

"Oh, why," Kerttu cried, "why didn't I heed poor Musti's warning!"

Suyettar dragged her roughly out of the water.

"Come along!" she said. "Dress yourself in those rags of mine and start that cake a-rolling! We ought to reach your brothers' house by to-night."

So poor Kerttu had to dress herself in Suyettar's filthy old garments while Suyettar, looking like a fresh young girl, decked herself out in Kerttu's pretty bodice and skirt.

Unwillingly now and with a heavy heart Kerttu threw down the cake and said:

>"Roll, roll, my little cake!
>Show me the way that I must take
>To find at last the brothers nine
>Whose own true mother is also mine!"

Off rolled the little cake and they two followed it, Kerttu weeping bitterly and Suyettar taunting her with ugly laughs. Then suddenly Kerttu forgot to weep for Suyettar took from her her memory and her tongue.

The little cake led them at last to a farmhouse before which it stopped. This was where the nine brothers were living. Eight of them were out working in the fields but the youngest was at home. He opened the door and when Suyettar told him that she was Kerttu, his sister, he kissed her tenderly and made her welcome. Then he invited her inside and they sat side by side on the bench and talked and Suyettar told him all she had heard from Kerttu about his mother and about the tokens which had been changed at Kerttu's birth. The youngest brother listened eagerly and Suyettar told her story so glibly that of course he supposed that she was his own true sister.

"And who is the awful looking old hag that has come with you?" he asked pointing at Kerttu.

"That? Oh, that's an old serving woman whom our mother sent with me to bear me company. She's dumb and foolish but she's a good herd and we can let her drive the cow out to pasture every day."

The older brothers when they came home were greatly pleased to find what they thought was their sister. They began to love her at once and to pet her and they said that now she must stay with them and keep house for them. She told them that was what she wanted to do and she said that now she was here the youngest brother need no longer stay at home but could go out every morning with the rest of them to work in the fields.

So now began a new life for poor Kerttu. In the

morning after the brothers were gone Suyettar would scold and abuse her. She would bake a cake for her dinner to be eaten in the fields and she would fill the cake with stones and sticks and filth. Then she would take Kerttu as far as the gate where she would give her back her tongue and her memory and order her roughly to drive the cow to pasture and look after it all day long. In the late afternoon when Kerttu drove home the cow, Suyettar would meet her at the gate and take from her her tongue and her memory and then in the evening the brothers would see her as a foolish old woman who couldn't talk. Every morning and every evening Kerttu begged Suyettar to show her a little mercy, but far from showing her any mercy Suyettar grew more cruel from day to day.

Suyettar was very proud to think that nine handsome young men took her for a beautiful girl and she felt sure they would never find out their mistake for only Kerttu knew who she really was and Kerttu was entirely in her power.

At night seated in the shadow in a far corner of the kitchen with her nine brothers laughing and talking Kerttu felt no sorrow for at such times of course she had no memory. But during the day it was different. Then when she was alone in the meadow she had her memory and her tongue and she thought about her poor mother at home anxiously awaiting her return and she thought of her nine sturdy brothers all of whom might now through her mistake fall victims to Suyettar. These thoughts made her weep with grief and as the days went by she put this grief into a song which she sang constantly:

> "I've found at last the brothers nine
> Whose own true mother is also mine,
> But they know me not from stick or stone!
> They leave me here to weep alone,
> While Suyettar sits in my place
> With stolen looks and stolen face!
> She snared me first with evil guile
> And now she mocks me all the while:
> By night she takes my tongue away,
> She feeds me sticks and stones by day! . . .
> Oh, little they guess, the brothers nine,
> That their own true mother is also mine!"

The brothers as they worked in nearby fields used to hear the song and they wondered about it.

"Strange!" they said to one another. "Can that be the old woman singing? In the evening at home she never opens her mouth and our dear sister always says that she's dumb and foolish."

One afternoon when Kerttu's song sounded particularly sad, the youngest brother crept close to the meadow where Kerttu was sitting in order to hear the words. He listened carefully and then hurried back to the others and with frightened face told them what he had heard.

"Nonsense!" the older brothers said. "It can't be so!"

However, they, too, wanted to hear for themselves the words of the strange song, so they all crept near to listen.

It looked like an old hag who was singing but the voice that came out of the withered mouth was the voice of a young girl. As they listened they, too, grew pale:

> "I've found at last the brothers nine
> Whose own true mother is also mine,
> But they know me not from stick or stone!
> They leave me here to weep alone,
> While Suyettar sits in my place
> With stolen looks and stolen face!
> She snared me first with evil guile
> And now she mocks me all the while:
> By night she takes my tongue away,
> She feeds me sticks and stones by day! . . .
> Oh, little they guess, the brothers nine,
> That their own true mother is also mine!"

"Can it be true?" they said, whispering together.

They sent the youngest brother to question Kerttu

and he, when he had heard her story, believed it true. Then the other brothers went to her one by one and questioned her and finally they were all convinced of the truth of her story.

"It is well for us," they said, "if we do not all fall into the power of that awful creature! How, O how can we rescue our poor little sister!"

"I can never get back my own looks," Kerttu said, "unless Suyettar splashes water into my eyes and unless I cry out a magic rime as she does it."

The brothers discussed one plan after another and at last agreed on one that they thought might deceive Suyettar.

They had Kerttu inflame her eyes with dust and come groping home one midday. The brothers, too, were at home and as Kerttu came stumbling into the kitchen they said to Suyettar:

"Oh, sister, sister, see the poor old woman! Something ails her! Her eyes—they're all red and swollen! Get some water and bathe them!"

"Nonsense!" Suyetter said. "The old hag's well enough! Let her be! She doesn't need any attention!"

"Oh, sister!" the youngest brother said, reproachfully, "is that any way for a human, kindhearted girl like you to talk? If you won't bathe the old creature's eyes, I will myself!"

Then Suyettar who of course wanted them to think that she was a human, kindhearted girl said, no, she would bathe them. So she took a basin of water over to Kerttu and told her to lean down her head. As she splashed the first drop of water into Kerttu's eyes, Kerttu cried out:

> "My own true looks give back to me
> And take your own for all to see!"

Instantly Suyettar was again a hideous old hag though still dressed in Kerttu's pretty bodice and skirt, and Kerttu was herself again, young and fresh and sweet, though still incased in Suyettar's rags. But the brothers pretended that they saw no difference and kept on talking to Suyettar as though they still thought her Kerttu. And Suyettar because her eyes were blinded with the dust supposed that they were still deceived.

Then one of the brothers said to Suyettar:

"Sister dear, the *sauna* is all heated and ready. Don't you want to bathe?"

Suyettar thought that this would be a fine chance to wash the dust from her eyes, so she let them lead her to the *sauna*. Once they got her inside they locked the door and set the *sauna* a-fire. Oh, the noise she made then when she found she had been trapped! She kicked and screamed and cursed and threatened! But Kerttu and the brothers paid no heed to her. They left her burning in the *sauna* while they hurried homewards.

They found their poor old mother seated at the window weeping, for she thought that now Kerttu as well as her sons was lost forever. As Kerttu and the nine handsome young men came in the gate she didn't recognize them until Kerttu sang out:

> "I bring at last the brothers nine
> Whose own true mother is also mine!"

Then she knew who they were and with thanks to God she welcomed them home.

THE FOREST BRIDE

The Story of a Little Mouse Who Was a Princess

THE FOREST BRIDE

There was once a farmer who had three sons. One day when the boys were grown to manhood he said to them:

"My sons, it is high time that you were all married. To-morrow I wish you to go out in search of brides."

"But where shall we go?" the oldest son asked.

"I have thought of that, too," the father said. "Do each of you chop down a tree and then take the direction in which the fallen tree points. I'm sure that each of you if you go far enough in that direction will find a suitable bride."

So the next day the three sons chopped down trees. The oldest son's tree fell pointing north.

"That suits me!" he said, for he knew that to the north lay a farm where a very pretty girl lived.

The tree of the second son when it fell pointed south.

"That suits me!" the second son declared thinking of

a girl that he had often danced with who lived on a farm to the south.

The youngest son's tree—the youngest son's name was Veikko—when it fell pointed straight to the forest.

"Ha! Ha!" the older brothers laughed. "Veikko will have to go courting one of the Wolf girls or one of the Foxes!"

They meant by this that only animals lived in the forest and they thought they were making a good joke at Veikko's expense. But Veikko said he was perfectly willing to take his chances and go where his tree pointed.

The older brothers went gaily off and presented their suits to the two farmers whose daughters they admired. Veikko, too, started off with brave front but after he had gone some distance in the forest his courage began to ebb.

"How can I find a bride," he asked himself, "in a place where there are no human creatures at all!"

Just then he came to a little hut. He pushed open the door and went in. It was empty. To be sure there was a little mouse sitting on the table, daintily combing her whiskers, but a mouse of course doesn't count.

"There's nobody here!" Veikko said aloud.

The little mouse paused in her toilet and turning towards him said reproachfully:

"Why, Veikko, I'm here!"

"But you don't count. You're only a mouse!"

"Of course I count!" the little mouse declared. "But tell me, what were you hoping to find?"

"I was hoping to find a sweetheart."

The little mouse questioned him further and Veikko told her the whole story of his brothers and the trees.

"The two older ones are finding sweethearts easily enough," Veikko said, "but I don't see how I can off here in the forest. And it will shame me to have to go home and confess that I alone have failed."

"See here, Veikko," the little mouse said, "why don't you take me for your sweetheart?"

Veikko laughed heartily.

"But you're only a mouse! Whoever heard of a man having a mouse for a sweetheart!"

The mouse shook her little head solemnly.

"Take my word for it, Veikko, you could do much worse than have me for a sweetheart! Even if I am only a mouse I can love you and be true to you."

She was a dear dainty little mouse and as she sat looking up at Veikko with her little paws under her chin and her bright little eyes sparkling Veikko liked her more and more.

Then she sang Veikko a pretty little song and the song

cheered him so much that he forgot his disappointment at not finding a human sweetheart and as he left her to go home he said:

"Very well, little mouse, I'll take you for my sweetheart!"

At that the mouse made little squeaks of delight and she told him that she'd be true to him and wait for him no matter how long he was in returning.

Well, the older brothers when they got home boasted loudly about their sweethearts.

"Mine," said the oldest, "has the rosiest reddest cheeks you ever saw!"

"And mine," the second announced, "has long yellow hair!"

Veikko said nothing.

"What's the matter, Veikko?" the older brothers asked him, laughing. "Has your sweetheart pretty pointed ears or sharp white teeth?"

You see they were still having their little joke about foxes and wolves.

"You needn't laugh," Veikko said. "I've found a sweetheart. She's a gentle dainty little thing gowned in velvet."

"Gowned in velvet!" echoed the oldest brother with a frown.

"Just like a princess!" the second brother sneered.

"Yes," Veikko repeated, "gowned in velvet like a princess. And when she sits up and sings to me I'm perfectly happy."

"Huh!" grunted the older brothers not at all pleased that Veikko should have so grand a sweetheart.

"Well," said the old farmer after a few days, "now I should like to know what those sweethearts of yours are able to do. Have them each bake me a loaf of bread so that I can see whether they're good housewives."

"Mine will be able to bake bread—I'm sure of that!" the oldest brother declared boastfully.

"So will mine!" chorused the second brother.

Veikko was silent.

"What about the Princess?" they said with a laugh. "Do you think the Princess can bake bread?"

"I don't know," Veikko answered truthfully. "I'll have to ask her."

Of course he had no reason for supposing that the little mouse could bake bread and by the time he reached the hut in the forest he was feeling sad and discouraged.

When he pushed open the door he found the little mouse as before seated on the table daintily combing her whiskers. At sight of Veikko she danced about with delight.

"I'm so glad to see you!" she squeaked. "I knew you would come back!"

Then when she noticed that he was silent she asked him what was the matter. Veikko told her:

"My father wants each of our sweethearts to bake him a loaf of bread. If I come home without a loaf my brothers will laugh at me."

"You won't have to go home without a loaf!" the little mouse said. "I can bake bread."

Veikko was much surprised at this.

"I never heard of a mouse that could bake bread!"

"Well, I can!" the little mouse insisted.

With that she began ringing a small silver bell, *tinkle, tinkle, tinkle.* Instantly there was the sound of hurrying footsteps, tiny scratchy footsteps, and hundreds of mice came running into the hut.

The little Princess mouse sitting up very straight and dignified said to them:

"Each of you go fetch me a grain of the finest wheat."

All the mice scampered quickly away and soon returned one by one, each carrying a grain of the finest wheat. After that it was no trick at all for the Princess mouse to bake a beautiful loaf of wheaten bread.

The next day the three brothers presented their father the loaves of their sweethearts' baking. The oldest one had a loaf of rye bread.

"Very good," the farmer said. "For hardworking people like us rye bread is good."

The loaf the second son had was made of barley.

"Barley bread is also good," the farmer said.

But when Veikko presented his loaf of beautiful wheaten bread, his father cried out:

"What! White bread! Ah, Veikko now must have a sweetheart of wealth!"

"Of course!" the older brothers sneered. "Didn't he tell us she was a Princess? Say, Veikko, when a Princess wants fine white flour, how does she get it?"

Veikko answered simply:

"She rings a little silver bell and when her servants come in she tells them to bring her grains of the finest wheat."

At this the older brothers nearly exploded with envy until their father had to reprove them.

"There! There!" he said. "Don't grudge the boy his good luck! Each girl has baked the loaf she knows how to make and each in her own way will probably make a good wife. But before you bring them home to me I want one further test of their skill in housewifery. Let them each send me a sample of their weaving."

The older brothers were delighted at this for they knew that their sweethearts were skilful weavers.

"We'll see how her ladyship fares this time!" they said, sure in their hearts that Veikko's sweetheart, whoever she was, would not put them to shame with her weaving.

Veikko, too, had serious doubts of the little mouse's ability at the loom.

"Whoever heard of a mouse that could weave?" he said to himself as he pushed open the door of the forest hut.

"Oh, there you are at last!" the little mouse squeaked joyfully.

She reached out her little paws in welcome and then in her excitement she began dancing about on the table.

"Are you really glad to see me, little mouse?" Veikko asked.

"Indeed I am!" the mouse declared. "Am I not your sweetheart? I've been waiting for you and waiting, just wishing that you would return! Does your father want something more this time, Veikko?"

"Yes, and it's something I'm afraid you can't give me, little mouse."

"Perhaps I can. Tell me what it is."

"It's a sample of your weaving. I don't believe you can weave. I never heard of a mouse that could weave."

"Tut! Tut!" said the mouse. "Of course I can weave! It would be a strange thing if Veikko's sweetheart couldn't weave!"

She rang the little silver bell, *tinkle, tinkle, tinkle,* and instantly there was the faint *scratch-scratch* of a hundred little feet as mice came running in from all directions and sat up on their haunches awaiting their Princess' orders.

"Go each of you," she said, "and get me a fiber of flax, the finest there is."

The mice went scurrying off and soon they began returning one by one each bringing a fiber of flax. When they had spun the flax and carded it, the little mouse wove a beautiful piece of fine linen. It was so sheer that she was able when she folded it to put it into an empty nutshell.

"Here, Veikko," she said, "here in this little box is a sample of my weaving. I hope your father will like it."

Veikko when he got home felt almost embarrassed for he was sure that his sweetheart's weaving would shame his brothers. So at first he kept the nutshell hidden in his pocket.

The sweetheart of the oldest brother had sent as a sample of her weaving a square of coarse cotton.

"Not very fine," the farmer said, "but good enough."

The second brother's sample was a square of cotton and linen mixed.

"A little better," the farmer said, nodding his head. Then he turned to Veikko.

"And you, Veikko, has your sweetheart not given you a sample of her weaving?"

Veikko handed his father a nutshell at sight of which his brothers burst out laughing.

"Ha! Ha! Ha!" they laughed. "Veikko's sweetheart gives him a nut when he asks for a sample of her weaving."

But their laughter died as the farmer opened the nutshell and began shaking out a great web of the finest linen.

"Why, Veikko, my boy!" he cried, "however did your sweetheart get threads for so fine a web?"

Veikko answered modestly:

"She rang a little silver bell and ordered her servants

to bring her in fibers of finest flax. They did so and after they had spun the flax and carded it, my sweetheart wove the web you see."

"Wonderful!" gasped the farmer. "I have never known such a weaver! The other girls will be all right for farmers' wives but Veikko's sweetheart might be a Princess! Well," concluded the farmer, "it's time that you all brought your sweethearts home. I want to see them with my own eyes. Suppose you bring them to-morrow."

"She's a good little mouse and I'm very fond of her," Veikko thought to himself as he went out to the forest, "but my brothers will certainly laugh when they find she is only a mouse! Well, I don't care if they do laugh! She's been a good little sweetheart to me and I'm not going to be ashamed of her!"

So when he got to the hut he told the little mouse at once that his father wanted to see her.

The little mouse was greatly excited.

"I must go in proper style!" she said.

She rang the little silver bell and ordered her coach and five. The coach when it came turned out to be an empty nutshell and the five prancing steeds that were drawing it were five black mice. The little mouse seated herself in the coach with a coachman mouse on the box in front of her and a footman mouse on the box behind her.

"Oh, how my brothers will laugh!" thought Veikko.

But he didn't laugh. He walked beside the coach and told the little mouse not to be frightened, that he would take good care of her. His father, he told her, was a gentle old man and would be kind to her.

When they left the forest they came to a river which was spanned by a foot bridge. Just as Veikko and the nutshell coach had reached the middle of the bridge, a man met them coming from the opposite direction.

"Mercy me!" the man exclaimed as he caught sight of the strange little coach that was rolling along beside Veikko. "What's that?"

He stooped down and looked and then with a loud laugh he put out his foot and pushed the coach, the little mouse, her servants, and her five prancing steeds —all off the bridge and into the water below.

"What have you done! What have you done!" Veikko cried. "You've drowned my poor little sweetheart!"

The man thinking Veikko was crazy hurried away.

Veikko with tears in his eyes looked down into the water.

"You poor little mouse!" he said. "How sorry I am

She beckoned to Veikko

THE FOREST BRIDE

that you are drowned! You were a faithful loving sweetheart and now that you are gone I know how much I loved you!"

As he spoke he saw a beautiful coach of gold drawn by five glossy horses go up the far bank of the river. A coachman in gold lace held the reins and a footman in pointed cap sat up stiffly behind. The most beautiful girl in the world was seated in the coach. Her skin was as red as a berry and as white as snow, her long golden hair gleamed with jewels, and she was dressed in pearly velvet. She beckoned to Veikko and when he came close she said:

"Won't you come sit beside me?"

"Me? Me?" Veikko stammered, too dazed to think.

The beautiful creature smiled.

"You were not ashamed to have me for a sweetheart when I was a mouse," she said, "and surely now that I am a Princess again you won't desert me!"

"A mouse!" Veikko gasped. "Were you the little mouse?"

The Princess nodded.

"Yes, I was the little mouse under an evil enchantment which could never have been broken if you had not taken me for a sweetheart and if another human being had not drowned me. Now the enchantment is broken forever. So come, we will go to your father and after he has given us his blessing we will get married and go home to my kingdom."

And that's exactly what they did. They drove at once to the farmer's house and when Veikko's father and his brothers and his brothers' sweethearts saw the Princess' coach stopping at their gate they all came out bowing and scraping to see what such grand folk could want of them.

"Father!" Veikko cried, "don't you know me?"

The farmer stopped bowing long enough to look up.

"Why, bless my soul!" he cried, "it's our Veikko!"

"Yes, father, I'm Veikko and this is the Princess that I'm going to marry!"

"A Princess, did you say, Veikko? Mercy me, where did my boy find a Princess?"

"Out in the forest where my tree pointed."

"Well, well, well," the farmer said, "where your tree pointed! I've always heard that was a good way to find a bride."

The older brothers shook their heads gloomily and muttered:

"Just our luck! If only our trees had pointed to the forest we, too, should have found princesses instead of plain country wenches!"

But they were wrong: it wasn't because his tree pointed to the forest that Veikko got the Princess, it was because he was so simple and good that he was kind even to a little mouse.

Well, after they had got the farmer's blessing they rode home to the Princess' kingdom and were married. And they were happy as they should have been for they were good and true to each other and they loved each other dearly.

THE ENCHANTED GROUSE

The Story of Helli and the Little Locked Box

THE ENCHANTED GROUSE

There was once an old couple who lived with their married son and his wife. The son's name was Helli. He was a dutiful son but his wife was a scold. She was always finding fault with the old people and with her husband and for that matter with everybody else as well.

One morning when she saw her husband taking out his bow and arrows she said:

"Where are you going now?"

"I'm going hunting," he told her.

"Isn't that just like you!" she cried. "You're going off to have a good time hunting and you don't give a thought to me who have to stay home alone with two stupid old people!"

"If I didn't go hunting," Helli said, "and shoot something, we'd have nothing to put in the pot for dinner and then you would have reason to scold."

At that the woman burst into tears.

"Of course, as usual blame me! Whatever happens it's my fault!"

Poor Helli hurried off, hoping that by the time he returned his wife would be in a calmer state of mind. He had small success with his hunting. He shot arrow after arrow but always missed his mark. Then when he had only one arrow left he saw a Grouse standing in some brushwood so near that there was little likelihood of his missing it.

He took good aim but before he could fire the Grouse said:

"Don't shoot me, brother! Take me home alive."

Helli paused, then he shook his head.

"I've got to shoot you for we've nothing to put in the pot for dinner."

Again he aimed his arrow and again the Grouse said:

"Don't shoot me, brother! Take me home alive."

For the second time Helli paused.

"I'd like to spare you," he said, "but what would my wife say if I came home empty-handed?"

He took aim again and a third time the Grouse said:

"Don't shoot me, brother! Take me home alive."

At that Helli dropped his arrow.

"I don't care what she says! I can't shoot a creature that begs so pitifully for its life! Very well, Mr.

Grouse, I'll do as you say: I'll take you home alive. But don't blame me if my wife wrings your neck."

He took the Grouse up in his arms and started homewards.

"Feed me for a year," the Grouse said, "and I'll reward you."

When they reached home and Helli's wife saw the Grouse, she cried out petulantly:

"Is that all you've got and out hunting all morning! That won't be dinner enough for four!"

"This Grouse isn't to be killed," Helli announced. "I'm going to keep it for a year and feed it."

"It won't take much to feed a Grouse," the old man remarked.

But the wife flew into a passion.

"What! Feed a useless bird when there isn't enough to feed your own flesh and blood!"

But Helli was firm and despite her threats his wife did not dare to maltreat the Grouse.

At the end of a year the Grouse grew a copper feather in its tail which it dropped in the dooryard. Then it disappeared.

"Ha!" laughed Helli's wife. "A copper feather! That's your reward for feeding that thankless bird a whole year! And now it's escaped!"

But the next day the Grouse returned.

"Feed me for another year," it said to Helli, "and I'll reward you."

His wife raised an awful to-do over this, but Helli was firm and for another year he fed and petted the Grouse.

At the end of the second year the Grouse grew a silver feather in its tail which it dropped in the dooryard. Then it disappeared.

"One silver feather!" Helli's wife cried. "So that's all you get for feeding that thankless bird a whole year! And now it's escaped!"

But it hadn't. It returned the very next day.

"Feed me for another year," it said to Helli, "and I'll reward you."

At the end of the third year the Grouse grew a golden feather in its tail and when it dropped that in the dooryard the scolding wife hadn't so much to say, for a golden feather was after all pretty good pay for a few handfuls of grain.

For a day the Grouse disappeared and then when it returned it said to Helli:

"Get on my back and I'll reward you."

Helli did so and the Grouse, rising high in the air, flew far away. On, on it flew until it reached the broad

On it flew until it reached the broad Ocean

Ocean. Over the Ocean it flew until Helli could see nothing but water in whatever direction he looked.

"Ha!" he said to himself with a shudder, "I hope I can hold on!"

As he spoke, the Grouse slipped from beneath him and he fell down, down, down. However, before he touched water the Grouse swooped under him and caught him up again high into the air. He had this same terrible experience a second time and a third time and each time he thought his last moment had arrived.

"Now," the Grouse told him, "you know what my feelings were when you threatened three times to shoot me with your arrow."

"You have taught me a lesson," Helli said.

After that the Grouse flew on and on. At last it said:

"Look straight ahead, master, and tell me what you see."

Helli shaded his eyes and looked.

"Far, far ahead I see what looks like a copper column."

"Good!" the Grouse said. "That is the home of my oldest sister. She will be overjoyed to see us and when she hears how you have spared my life she will want to make you a present and will offer you various things. Take my advice and tell her that the only thing you want is her little locked box the key to which is lost. If she won't give you that, accept nothing."

The Grouse's oldest sister received them most hospitably and when she had heard their story at once offered Helli anything he might like from among her treasures.

"Then give me your little locked box the key to which is lost," Helli said.

The oldest sister shook her head.

"My little locked box! Who told you about that? I'm sorry, but I cannot give you that! Take anything else!"

"No," Helli said, "that or nothing!"

When the oldest sister could not be prevailed upon to give away her little locked box, the Grouse had Helli mount his back once more and off they flew.

"We'll visit my second sister now," he said. "If she offers you a present, ask her for her little locked box without a key and accept nothing else."

On, on they flew until the oldest sister's castle was far behind.

"Look, master," the Grouse said, "look straight ahead and tell me what you see."

Helli shaded his eyes and looked.

"Far ahead I see something that is like a silver cloud."

"That," said the Grouse, "is the silver castle of my second sister."

At the silver castle the second sister received them with joy and when she heard who Helli was at once declared that she wanted to show him her gratitude by making him a gift.

"Ask from me what you will," she said, "and you shall have it."

But when he asked for her little locked box without a key, she cried out:

"No! No! Not that! Anything else!"

"But I don't want anything else!" Helli said.

When the Grouse saw that his second sister was not to be parted from her little locked box, he bade Helli mount his back and off they flew again.

"We'll go to my youngest sister this time," he said. "If she offers you a present, ask for the same thing."

On, on they flew until the silver castle was lost to view.

"Now, master, look ahead and tell me what you see."

Helli shaded his eyes and looked.

"I seem to see a golden haze like the sun behind a cloud."

"That is the golden castle of my youngest sister."

They arrived and the youngest sister threw her arms about the Grouse for she loved him dearly and had not seen him for a long time.

"Welcome, brother!" she said. "And welcome also to you, Helli!"

Then she offered Helli a present and when he asked for her little locked box without a key she gave it to him at once.

"It is my most precious possession," she said, "but you may have it for you spared my dear brother's life when you might have taken it."

After they had rested and feasted they bade the youngest sister farewell and Helli with his precious box held tightly in one hand mounted the Grouse's back and off they flew towards home.

"Be careful of the box," the Grouse said, "and don't let it out of your hands until we reach some beautiful spot where you'd like always to live."

They passed high mountains and wooded lakes and fertile valleys.

"Shall we stop here?" the Grouse asked. "Or here? Or here?"

But always Helli said:

"No, not here."

At last they reached home and the Grouse told Helli that now they must part forever.

"By sparing my life three times," the Grouse said, "and then feeding me for three years you have broken the enchantment that bound me and now I shall not have to go about any longer as a grouse but shall be able to resume my natural shape. Farewell, Helli, and when you find the spot where you think you would like always to live, drop the box and you will find you have a treasure that will more than reward you for your kindness to me."

The Grouse disappeared and Helli said to himself:

"Where do I want to live always but right here at home with my dear old father and mother and my wife who is my wife even if she does scold me sometimes!"

So there at home after they all had supper together, he dropped the box on the floor. It broke and out of it arose a beautiful castle with servants and riches and everything that Helli had always wanted and never had. And Helli and his old father and mother and his wife lived in it and were happy. And gradually his wife got over her habit of scolding for when you're happy you haven't anything to scold about.

THE TERRIBLE OLLI

The Story of an Honest Finn and a Wicked Troll

THE TERRIBLE OLLI

There was once a wicked rich old Troll who lived on a Mountain that sloped down to a Bay. A decent Finn, a farmer, lived on the opposite side of the Bay. The farmer had three sons. When the boys had reached manhood he said to them one day:

"I should think it would shame you three strong youths that that wicked old Troll over there should live on year after year and no one trouble him. We work hard like honest Finns and are as poor at the end of the year as at the beginning. That old Troll with all his wickedness grows richer and richer. I tell you, if you boys had any real spirit you'd take his riches from him and drive him away!"

His youngest son, whose name was Olli, at once cried out:

"Very well, father, I will!"

But the two older sons, offended at Olli's promptness, declared:

"You'll do no such thing! Don't forget your place in the family! You're the youngest and we're not going to let you push us aside. Now, father, we two will go across the Bay and rout out that old Troll. Olli may come with us if he likes and watch us while we do it."

Olli laughed and said: "All right!" for he was used to his brothers treating him like a baby.

So in a few days the three brothers walked around the Bay and up the Mountain and presented themselves at the Troll's house. The Troll and his old wife were both at home. They received the brothers with great civility.

"You're the sons of the Finn who lives across the Bay, aren't you?" the Troll said. "I've watched you boys grow up. I am certainly glad to see you for I have three daughters who need husbands. Marry my daughters and you'll inherit my riches."

The old Troll made this offer in order to get the young men into his power.

"Be careful!" Olli whispered.

But the brothers were too delighted at the prospect of inheriting the Troll's riches so easily to pay any heed to Olli's warning. Instead they accepted the Troll's offer at once.

Well, the old Troll's wife made them a fine supper and after supper the Troll sent them to bed with his three daughters. But first he put red caps on the three youths and white caps on the three Troll girls. He made a joke about the caps.

"A red cap and a white cap in each bed!" he said.

The older brothers suspected nothing and soon fell asleep. Olli, too, pretended to fall asleep and when he was sure that none of the Troll girls were still awake he got up and quietly changed the caps. He put the white caps on himself and his brothers and the red caps on the Troll girls. Then he crept back to bed and waited.

Presently the old Troll came over to the beds with a long knife in his hand. There was so little light in the room that he couldn't see the faces of the sleepers, but it was easy enough to distinguish the white caps from the red caps. With three swift blows he cut off the heads under the red caps, thinking of course they were the heads of the three Finnish youths. Then he went back to bed with the old Troll wife and Olli could hear them both chuckling and laughing. After a time they went soundly to sleep as Olli could tell from their deep regular breathing and their loud snores.

Olli now roused his brothers and told them what had

happened and the three of them slipped quietly out of the Troll house and hurried home to their father on the other side of the Bay.

After that the older brothers no longer talked of despoiling the Troll. They didn't care to try another encounter with him.

"He might have cut our heads off!" they said, shuddering to think of the awful risk they had run.

Olli laughed at them.

"Come on!" he kept saying to them day after day. "Let's go across the Bay to the Troll's!"

"We'll do no such thing!" they told him. "And you wouldn't suggest it either if you weren't so young and foolish!"

"Well," Olli announced at last, "if you won't come with me I'm going alone. I've heard that the Troll has a horse with hairs of gold and silver. I've decided I want that horse."

"Olli," his father said, "I don't believe you ought to go. You know what your brothers say. That old Troll is an awfully sly one!"

But Olli only laughed.

"Good-by!" he called back as he waved his hand. "When you see me again I'll be riding the Troll's horse!"

Olli and the Troll's horse

The Troll wasn't at home but the old Troll wife was there. When she saw Olli she thought to herself:

"Mercy me, here's that Finnish boy again, the one that changed the caps! What shall I do? I must keep him here on some pretext or other until the Troll comes home!"

So she pretended to be very glad to see him.

"Why, Olli," she said, "is that you? Come right in!"

She talked to him as long as she could and when she could think of nothing more to say she asked him would he take the horse and water it at the Lake.

"That will keep him busy," she thought to herself, "and long before he gets back from the Lake the Troll will be here."

But Olli, instead of leading the horse down to the Lake, jumped on its back and galloped away. By the time the Troll reached home, he was safely on the other side of the Bay.

When the Troll heard from the old Troll wife what had happened, he went down to the shore and hallooed across the Bay:

"Olli! Oh, Olli, are you there?"

Olli made a trumpet of his hands and called back:

"Yes, I'm here! What do you want?"

"Olli, have you got my horse?"

"Yes, I've got your horse but it's my horse now!"

"Olli! Olli!" his father cried. "You mustn't talk that way to the Troll! You'll make him angry!"

And his brothers looking with envy at the horse with gold and silver hairs warned him sourly:

"You better be careful, young man, or the Troll will get you yet!"

A few days later Olli announced:

"I think I'll go over and get the Troll's money-bag."

His father tried to dissuade him.

"Don't be foolhardy, Olli! Your brothers say you had better not go to the Troll's house again."

But Olli only laughed and started gaily off as though he hadn't a fear in the world.

Again he found the old Troll wife alone.

"Mercy me!" she thought to herself as she saw him coming, "here is that terrible Olli again! Whatever shall I do? I mustn't let him off this time before the Troll gets back! I must keep him right here with me in the house."

So when he came in she pretended that she was tired and that her back ached and she asked him would he watch the bread in the oven while she rested a few moments on the bed.

"Certainly I will," Olli said.

So the old Troll wife lay down on the bed and Olli sat quietly in front of the oven. The Troll wife really was tired and before she knew it she fell asleep.

"Ha!" thought Olli, "here's my chance!"

Without disturbing the Troll wife he reached under the bed, pulled out the big money-bag full of silver pieces, threw it over his shoulder, and hurried home.

He was measuring the money when he heard the Troll hallooing across to him:

"Olli! Oh, Olli, are you there?"

"Yes," Olli shouted back, "I'm here! What do you want?"

"Olli, have you got my money-bag?"

"Yes, I've got your money-bag but it's my money-bag now!"

A few days later Olli said:

"Do you know, the Troll has a beautiful coverlet woven of silk and gold. I think I'll go over and get it."

His father as usual protested but Olli laughed at him merrily and went. He took with him an auger and a can of water. He hid until it was dark, then climbed the roof of the Troll's house and bored a hole right over the bed. When the Troll and his wife went to sleep he sprinkled some water on the coverlet and on their faces.

The Troll woke with a start.

"I'm wet!" he said, "and the bed's wet, too!"

The old Troll wife got up to change the covers.

"The roof must be leaking," she said. "It never leaked before. I suppose it was that last wind."

She threw the wet coverlet up over the rafters to dry and put other covers on the bed.

When she and the Troll were again asleep, Olli made the hole a little bigger, reached in his hand, and got the coverlet from the rafters.

The next morning the Troll hallooed across the Bay:

"Olli! Oh, Olli, are you there?"

"Yes," Ollie shouted back, "I'm here! What do you want?"

"Have you got my coverlet woven of silk and gold?"

"Yes," Olli told him, "I've got your coverlet but it's my coverlet now!"

A few days later Olli said:

"There's still one thing in the Troll's house that I think I ought to get. It's a golden bell. If I get that golden bell then there will be nothing left that had better belong to an honest Finn."

So he went again to the Troll's house taking with him a saw and an auger. He hid until night and, when the Troll and his wife were asleep, he cut a hole through the side of the house through which he reached in his hand to get the bell. At the touch of his hand the bell tinkled and woke the Troll. The Troll jumped out of bed and grabbed Olli's hand.

"Ha! Ha!" he cried. "I've got you now and this time you won't get away!"

Olli didn't try to get away. He made no resistance while the Troll dragged him into the house.

"We'll eat him—that's what we'll do!" the Troll said to his wife. "Heat the oven at once and we'll roast him!"

So the Troll wife built a roaring fire in the oven.

"He'll make a fine roast!" the Troll said, pinching Olli's arms and legs. "I think we ought to invite the other Troll folk to come and help us eat him up. Suppose I just go over the Mountain and gather them in. You can manage here without me. As soon as the oven is well heated just take Olli and slip him in and close the door and by the time we come he'll be done."

"Very well," the Troll wife said, "but don't be too long! He's young and tender and will roast quickly!"

So the Troll went out to invite to the feast the Troll folk who lived on the other side of the Mountain and Olli was left alone with the Troll wife.

When the oven was well heated she raked out the coals and said to Olli:

"Now then, my boy, sit down in front of the oven with your back to the opening and I'll push you in nicely."

Olli pretended he didn't quite understand. He sat down first one way and then another, spreading himself out so large that he was too big for the oven door.

"Not that way!" the Troll wife kept saying. "Hunch up little, straight in front of the door!"

"You show me how," Olli begged.

So the old Troll wife sat down before the oven directly in front of the opening, and she hunched herself up very compactly with her chin on her knees and her arms around her legs.

"Oh, that way!" Olli said, "so that you can just take hold of me and push me in and shut the door!"

And as he spoke he took hold of her and pushed her in and slammed the door! And that was the end of the old Troll wife!

Olli let her roast in the oven until she was done to a turn. Then he took her out and put her on the table all ready for the feast.

Then he filled a sack with straw and dressed the sack up in some of the old Troll wife's clothes. He threw the dressed up sack on the bed and, just to glance at it, you'd suppose it was the Troll wife asleep.

Then Olli took the golden bell and went home.

Well, presently the Troll and all the Troll folk from over the Mountain came trooping in.

"Yum! Yum! It certainly smells good!" they said as they got the first whiff from the big roast on the table.

"See!" the Troll said, pointing to the bed. "The old woman's asleep! Well, let her sleep! She's tired! We'll just sit down without her!"

So they set to and feasted and feasted.

"Ha! Ha!" said the Troll. "This is the way to serve a troublesome young Finn!"

Just then his knife struck something hard and he looked down to see what it was.

"Mercy me!" he cried, "if here isn't one of the old woman's beads! What can that mean? You don't suppose the roast is not Olli after all but the old woman! No! No! It can't be!"

He got up and went over to the bed. Then he came back shaking his head sadly.

"My friends," he said, "we've been eating the old woman! However, we've eaten so much of her that I suppose we might as well finish her!"

So the Troll folk sat all night feasting and drinking.

At dawn the Troll went down to the water and hallooed across:

"Olli! Oh, Olli, are you there?"

Olli who was safely home shouted back:

"Yes, I'm here! What do you want?"

"Have you got my golden bell?"

"Yes, I've got your golden bell but it's my golden bell now!"

"One thing more, Olli: did you roast my old woman?"

"Your old woman?" Olli echoed. "Look! Is that she?"

Olli pointed at the rising sun which was coming up behind the Troll.

The Troll turned and looked. He looked straight at the sun and then, of course, he burst!

So that was the end of him!

Well, after that no other Troll ever dared settle on that side of the Mountain. They were all too afraid of the Terrible Olli!

THE DEVIL'S HIDE

The Story of the Boy Who Wouldn't Lose His Temper

THE DEVIL'S HIDE

There was once a Finnish boy who got the best of the Devil. His name was Erkki. Erkki had two brothers who were, of course, older than he. They both tried their luck with the Devil and got the worst of it. Then Erkki tried his luck. They were sure Erkki, too, would be worsted, but he wasn't. Here is the whole story:

One day the oldest brother said:

"It's time for me to go out into the world and earn my living. Do you two younger ones wait here at home until you hear how I get on."

The younger boys agreed to this and the oldest brother started out. He was unable to get employment until by chance he met the Devil. The Devil at once offered him a place but on very strange terms.

"Come work for me," the Devil said, "and I promise that you'll be comfortably housed and well fed. We'll make this bargain: the first of us who loses his temper will forfeit to the other enough of his own hide to sole a pair of boots. If I lose my temper first, you may exact from me a big patch of my hide. If you lose your temper first, I'll exact the same from you."

The oldest brother agreed to this and the Devil at once took him home and set him to work.

"Take this ax," he said, "and go out behind the house and chop me some firewood."

The oldest brother took the ax and went out to the woodpile.

"Chopping wood is easy enough," he thought to himself.

But at the first blow he found that the ax had no edge. Try as he would he couldn't cut a single log.

"I'd be a fool to stay here and waste my time with such an ax!" he cried.

So he threw down the ax and ran away thinking to escape the Devil and get work somewhere else. But the Devil had no intention of letting him escape. He ran after him, overtook him, and asked him what he meant leaving thus without notice.

"I don't want to work for you!" the oldest brother cried, petulantly.

"Very well," the Devil said, "but don't lose your temper about it."

"I will so lose my temper!" the oldest brother declared. "The idea—expecting me to cut wood with such an ax!"

"Well," the Devil remarked, "since you insist on losing your temper, you'll have to forfeit me enough of your hide to sole a pair of boots! That was our bargain."

The oldest brother howled and protested but to no purpose. The Devil was firm. He took out a long knife and slit off enough of the oldest brother's hide to sole a pair of big boots.

"Now then, my boy," he said, "now you may go."

The oldest brother went limping home complaining bitterly at the hard fate that had befallen him.

"I'm tired and sick," he told his brothers, "and I'm going to stay home and rest. One of you will have to go out and get work."

The second brother at once said that he'd be delighted to try his luck in the world. So he started out and he had exactly the same experience. At first he could get no work, then he met the Devil and the Devil made exactly the same bargain with him that he had made with the oldest brother. He took the second brother home with him, gave him the same dull ax, and sent him out to the woodpile. After the first stroke the second brother threw down the ax in disgust and tried to run off and the Devil, of course, wouldn't let him go until he, too, had submitted to the loss of a great patch of hide. So it was no time at all before the second brother came limping home complaining bitterly at fate.

"What ails you two?" Erkki said.

"You go out into the cruel world and hunt work," they told him, "and you'll find out soon enough what ails us! And when you do find out you needn't come limping home expecting sympathy from us for you won't get it!"

So the very next day Erkki started out, leaving his brothers at home nursing their sore backs and their injured feelings.

Well, Erkki had exactly the same experience. At first he could get work nowhere, then later he met the Devil and went into his employ on exactly the same terms as his brothers.

The Devil handed him the same dull ax and sent him out to the woodpile. At the first blow Erkki knew that the ax had lost its edge and would never cut a single log. But instead of being discouraged and losing his temper, he only laughed.

"I suppose the Devil thinks I'll lose my hide over a trifle like this!" he said. "Well, I just won't!"

He dropped the ax and, going over to the woodpile, began pulling it down. Under all the logs he found the Devil's cat. It was an evil looking creature with a gray head.

"Ha!" thought Erkki, "I bet anything you've got something to do with this!"

He raised the dull ax and with one blow cut off the evil creature's head. Sure enough the ax instantly recovered its edge and after that Erkki had no trouble at all in chopping as much firewood as the Devil wanted.

That night at supper the Devil said:

"Well, Erkki, did you finish the work I gave you?"

"Yes, master, I've chopped all that wood."

The Devil was surprised.

"Really?"

"Yes, master. You can go out and see for yourself."

"Then you found something in the woodpile, didn't you?"

"Nothing but an awful looking old cat."

The Devil started.

"Did you do anything to that cat?"

"I only chopped its head off and threw it away."

"What!" the Devil cried angrily. "Didn't you know that was my cat!"

"There now, master," Erkki said soothingly, "you're

not going to lose your temper over a little thing like a dead cat, are you? Don't forget our bargain!"

The Devil swallowed his anger and murmured:

"No, I'm not going to lose my temper but I must say that was no way to treat my cat."

The next day the Devil ordered Erkki to go out to the forest and bring home some logs on the ox sledge.

"My black dog will go with you," he said, "and as you come home you're to take exactly the same course the dog takes."

Well, Erkki went out to the forest and loaded the ox sledge with logs and then drove the oxen home following the Devil's black dog. As they reached the Devil's house the black dog jumped through a hole in the gate.

"I must follow master's orders," Erkki said to himself.

So he cut up the oxen into small pieces and put them through the same hole in the gate; he chopped up the logs and pitched them through the hole; and he broke up the sledge into pieces small enough to follow the oxen and the logs. Then he crept through the hole himself.

That night at supper the Devil said:

"Well, Erkki, did you come home the way I told you?"

"Yes, master, I followed the black dog."

"What!" the Devil cried. "Do you mean to say you brought the oxen and the sledge and the logs through the hole in the gate?"

"Yes, master, that's what I did."

"But you couldn't!" the Devil declared.

"Well, master," Erkki said, "just go out and see."

The Devil went outside and when he saw the method by which Erkki had carried out his orders he was furious. But Erkki quieted him by saying:

"There now, master, you're not going to lose your temper over a trifling matter like this, are you? Remember our bargain!"

"N-n-no," the Devil said, again swallowing his anger, "I'm not going to lose my temper, but I want you to understand, Erkki, that I think you've acted very badly in this!"

All that evening the Devil fumed and fussed about Erkki.

"We've got to get rid of that boy! That's all there is about it!" he said to his wife.

Of course whenever Erkki was in sight the Devil

tried to smile and look pleasant, but as soon as Erkki was gone he went back at once to his grievance. He declared emphatically:

"There's no living in peace and comfort with such a boy around!"

"Well," his wife said, "if you feel that way about it, why don't you kill him to-night when he's asleep? We could throw his body into the lake and no one be the wiser."

"That's a fine idea!" the Devil said. "Wake me up some time after midnight and I'll do it!"

Now Erkki overheard this little plan, so that night he kept awake. When he knew from their snoring that the Devil and his wife were sound asleep, he slipped over to their bed, quietly lifted the Devil's wife in his arms, and without awakening her placed her gently in his own bed. Then he put on some of her clothes and laid himself down beside the Devil in the wife's place.

Presently he nudged the Devil awake.

"What do you want?" the Devil mumbled.

"Sst!" Erkki whispered. "Isn't it time we got up and killed Erkki?"

"Yes," the Devil answered, "it is. Come along."

They got up quietly and the Devil reached down a great sword from the wall. Then they crept over to

Erkki's bed and the Devil with one blow cut off the head of the person who was lying there asleep.

"Now," he said, "we'll just carry out the bed and all and dump it in the lake."

So Erkki took one end of the bed and the Devil the other and, stumbling and slipping in the darkness, they carried it down to the lake and pitched it in.

"That's a good job done!" the Devil said with a laugh.

Then they went back to bed together and the Devil fell instantly asleep.

The next morning when he got up for breakfast, there was Erkki stirring the porridge.

"How—did you get here?" the Devil asked. "I mean—I mean where is my wife?"

"Your wife? Don't you remember," Erkki said, "you cut off her head last night and then we threw her into the lake, bed and all! But no one will be the wiser!"

"W-wh-what!" the Devil cried, and he was about to fly into an awful rage when Erkki restrained him by saying:

"There now, master, you're not going to lose your temper over a little thing like a wife, are you? Remember our bargain!"

So the Devil was forced again to swallow his anger.

"No, I'm not going to lose my temper," he said, "but I tell you frankly, Erkki, I don't think that was a nice trick for you to play on me!"

Well, the Devil felt lonely not having a wife about the house, so in a few days he decided to go off wooing for a new one.

"And, Erkki," he said, "I expect you to keep busy while I'm gone. Here's a keg of red paint. Now get to work and have the house all blazing red by the time I get back."

"All blazing red," Erkki repeated. "Very well, master, trust me to have it all blazing red by the time you get back!"

As soon as the Devil was gone, Erkki set the house a-fire and in a short time the whole sky was lighted up with the red glow of the flames. In great fright the Devil hurried back and got there in time to see the house one mass of fire.

"You see, master," Erkki said, "I've done as you told me. It looks very pretty, doesn't it? all blazing red!"

The Devil almost choked with rage.

"You—you—" he began, but Erkki restrained him by saying:

"There now, master, you're not going to lose your

From the bones of the cattle he laid three bridges

THE DEVIL'S HIDE

temper over a little thing like a house a-fire, are you? Remember our bargain!"

The Devil swallowed hard and said:

"N—no, I'm not going to lose my temper, but I must say, Erkki, that I'm very much annoyed with you!"

The next day the Devil wanted to go a-wooing again and before he started he said to Erkki:

"Now, no nonsense this time! While I'm gone you're to build three bridges over the lake, but they're not to be built of wood or stone or iron or earth. Do you understand?"

Erkki pretended to be frightened.

"That's a pretty hard task you've given me, master!"

"Hard or easy, see that you get it done!" the Devil said.

Erkki waited until the Devil was gone, then he went out to the field and slaughtered all the Devil's cattle. From the bones of the cattle he laid three bridges across the lake, using the skulls for one bridge, the ribs for another, and the legs and the hoofs for the third. Then when the Devil got back, Erkki met him and pointing to the bridges said:

"See, master, there they are, three bridges put together without stick, stone, iron, or bit of earth!"

When the Devil found out that all his cattle had been slaughtered to give bones for the bridges, he was ready to kill Erkki, but Erkki quieted him by saying:

"There now, master, you're not going to lose your temper over a little thing like the slaughter of a few cattle, are you? Remember our bargain!"

So again the Devil had to swallow his anger.

"No," he said, "I'm not going to lose my temper exactly but I just want to tell you, Erkki, that I don't think you're behaving well!"

The Devil's wooing was successful and pretty soon he brought home a new wife. The new wife didn't like having Erkki about, so the Devil promised her he'd kill the boy.

"I'll do it to-night," he said, "when he's asleep."

Erkki overheard this and that night he put the churn in his bed under the covers, and where his head ordinarily would be he put a big round stone. Then he himself curled up on the stove and went comfortably to sleep.

During the night the Devil took his great sword from the wall and went over to Erkki's bed. His first blow hit the round stone and nicked the sword. His second blow struck sparks.

"Mercy me!" the Devil thought, "he's got a mighty hard head! I better strike lower!"

With the third stroke he hit the churn a mighty blow. The hoops flew apart and the churn collapsed.

The Devil went chuckling back to bed.

"Ha!" he said boastfully to his wife, "I got him that time!"

But the next morning when he woke up he didn't feel like laughing for there was Erkki as lively as ever and pretending that nothing had happened.

"What!" cried the Devil in amazement, "didn't you feel anything strike you last night while you were asleep?"

"Oh, I did feel a few mosquitoes brushing my cheek," Erkki said. "Nothing else."

"Steel doesn't touch him!" the Devil said to his wife. "I think I'll try fire on him."

So that night the Devil told Erkki to sleep in the threshing barn. Erkki carried his cot down to the threshing floor and then when it was dark he shifted it into the hay barn where he slept comfortably all night.

During the night the Devil set fire to the threshing barn. In the early dawn Erkki carried his cot back to the place of the threshing barn and in the morning when the Devil came out the first thing he saw was Erkki unharmed and peacefully sleeping among the smoking ruins.

"Mercy me, Erkki!" he shouted, shaking him awake, "have you been asleep all night?"

Erkki sat up and yawned.

"Yes, I've had a fine night's sleep. But I did feel a little chilly."

"Chilly!" the Devil gasped.

After that the Devil's one thought was to get rid of Erkki.

"That boy's getting on my nerves!" he told his wife. "I just can't stand him much longer! What are we going to do about him?"

They discussed one plan after another and at last decided that the only way they'd ever get rid of him would be to move away and leave him behind.

"I'll send him out to the forest to chop wood all day," the Devil said, "and while he's gone we'll row ourselves and all our belongings out to an island and when he comes back he won't know where we've gone."

Erkki overheard this plan and the next day when they were sure he was safely at work in the forest he slipped back and hid himself in the bedclothes.

Well, when they got to the island and began unpacking their things there was Erkki in the bedclothes!

The Devil's new wife complained bitterly.

"If you really loved me," she said, "you'd cut off that boy's head!"

"But I've tried to cut it off!" the Devil declared, "and I never can do it! Plague take such a boy! I've always known the Finns were an obstinate lot but I must say I've never met one as bad as Erkki! He's too much for me!"

But the Devil's wife kept on complaining until at last the Devil promised that he would try once again to cut off Erkki's head.

"Very well," his wife said, "to-night when he's asleep I'll wake you."

Well, what with the moving and everything the wife herself was tired and as soon as she went to bed she fell asleep. That gave Erkki just the very chance he needed to try on the new wife the trick he had played on the old one. Without waking her he carried her to his bed and then laid himself down in her place beside the Devil. Then he waked up the Devil and reminded him that he had promised to cut off Erkki's head.

The poor old Devil got up and went over to Erkki's bed and of course cut off the head of his new wife.

The next morning when he had found out what he had done, he was perfectly furious.

"You get right out of here, Erkki!" he roared. "I never want to see you again!"

"There now, master," Erkki said, "you're not going to lose your temper over a little thing like a dead wife, are you?"

"I am so going to lose my temper!" the Devil shouted. "And what's more it isn't a little thing! I liked this wife, I did, and I don't know where I'll get another one I like as well! So you just clear out of here and be quick about it, too!"

"Very well, master," Erkki said, "I'll go but not until you pay me what you owe me."

"What I owe you!" bellowed the Devil. "What about all you owe me for my house and my cattle and my old wife and my dear new wife and everything!"

"You've lost your temper," Erkki said, "and now you've got to pay me a patch of your hide big enough to sole a pair of boots. That was our bargain!"

The Devil roared and blustered but Erkki was firm. He wouldn't budge a step until the Devil had allowed him to slit a great patch of hide off his back.

That piece of the Devil's hide made the finest soles that a pair of boots ever had. It wore for years and

THE DEVIL'S HIDE

years and years. In fact Erkki is still tramping around on those same soles. The fame of them has spread over all the land and it has got so that now people stop Erkki on the highway to look at his wonderful boots soled with the Devil's hide. Travelers from foreign countries are deeply interested when they hear about the boots and when they meet Erkki they question him closely.

"Tell us," they beg him, "how did you get the Devil's hide in the first place?"

Erkki always laughs and makes the same answer:

"I got it by not losing my temper!"

As for the Devil, he's never again made a bargain like that with a Finn!

THE MYSTERIOUS SERVANT

*The Story of a Young Man Who Respected
the Dead*

THE MYSTERIOUS SERVANT

There was once a rich merchant who had an only son. As he lay dying, he said:

"Matti, my boy, my end is approaching and there are two things I want to say to you: The first is that I am leaving you all my wealth. If you are careful you will have enough to suffice you for life. The second thing I have to say is to beg you never to leave this, your native village. At your birth there was a prophecy which declared that if ever you left this village you would have to marry a woman with horns. Now that I have warned you in time it will be your own fault if ever you have to meet this fate."

The merchant died and Matti was left alone. He had never before wanted to travel but now that he knew of the fate which would overtake him if he did, he couldn't bear the thought of remaining forever a prisoner in his native village.

"What is the use of riches," he asked himself, "if one can't travel over the broad world and see wonderful sights? Besides, if it's my fate to marry a horned woman, I don't see why sitting quietly at home is going to save me. No! I'm going to take my chances like a man and come and go as I like!"

So he gathered his riches together, closed the old house where he had been born, and started out into the bright world. He traveled many days, meeting strange peoples and seeing strange sights. At last he settled down in a large city and became a merchant like his father.

One afternoon as he was out walking, he saw a crowd of men dragging the body of a dead man in the gutter. They were kicking and abusing the dead body, and calling it evil names.

Matti stopped them.

"What is this you are doing?" he demanded. "Don't you know that disrespect to the dead is disrespect to God? Give over abusing this poor dead body and bury it decently or God will punish you!"

"Let us alone!" the men cried. "He deserves the abuse we are giving him! When he was alive he borrowed money from us all and then he died without repaying us. Are we to have no satisfaction at all?"

THE MYSTERIOUS SERVANT 197

With that they resumed their abuse of the dead body.

"Wait!" Matti cried. "Tell me what the dead man owed you and I will pay it!"

"He owed me ten ducats!" said one.

"And me a hundred!" shouted another.

"And me five hundred!"

"And me a thousand!"

"Come all of you to my house," Matti said, "and I will pay you, but only on condition that first you hand over the body to me and help me give it a decent burial."

The men agreed. They helped Matti bury the dead man and then went home with him.

Each told Matti the amount the dead man owed him and, true to his promise, Matti paid them all.

When he had paid the last man he found that he had nothing left for himself but nine silver kopeks. The dead man's debts had exhausted all the wealth his father had left him.

"No matter!" Matti thought to himself. "My riches would have done me no good if I had stood by and allowed a poor dead man to be abused. What if I have nothing left? I'm young and strong and I can go out into the world and make my livelihood somehow. I'll go home and have one last look at my native village and then begin life anew."

So, dressed in shabby old clothes with nothing in his pockets but the nine silver kopeks, Matti left the city where people were beginning to know him as a merchant and started back to his native village. He was soon met by a man who addressed him respectfully and asked to be engaged as his servant.

"My servant!" Matti repeated with a laugh. "My dear fellow, I'm too poor to have a servant! All I have in the world are nine silver kopeks!"

"No matter, master," the man said. "Take me anyhow. I will serve you well and I promise you will not regret our bargain."

So Matti agreed and they walked on together. The sun was hot and by midafternoon Matti was feeling faint with hunger and fatigue.

"Master," the Servant said, "I will run ahead to the next village and order the landlord at the inn to prepare you a fine dinner. Do you come along slowly and by the time you arrive the dinner will be ready."

"But remember," Mattie warned him, "I have no money to pay for a fine dinner!"

"Trust me!" the Servant said and off he hurried.

At the next village he hunted out the best inn and ordered the landlord to prepare his finest dinner without delay. He was so particular that everything should be the best that the landlord supposed his master must be some great lord.

When Matti arrived on foot, tired and travel-stained and shabby, the landlord was amazed.

"It's fine lords we have nowadays!" he muttered scornfully, and he wished he had not been in such haste to cook the best food in the house. But it was cooked and ready to serve and so, with an ill grace, he served it.

Matti and his man ate their fill of good cabbage soup and fish and fowl tender and juicy.

It quite enraged the landlord to see poor men with such good appetites.

"They eat as if their pockets were lined with gold!" he muttered angrily. "Well, let them eat while they can for they'll lose their appetites once they see the reckoning!"

When they finished eating, they rested and then called for the reckoning. It was much more than it should have been but neither Matti nor the Servant objected.

"Like a good fellow," the Servant said, "will you please to lend me your half peck measure."

"Like a good fellow, indeed!" the landlord muttered to himself. "Who are you to call me a good fellow I'd like to know!"

Nevertheless he went out and got the measure.

"Now, master," the Servant said, "give me three of your nine silver kopeks."

The Servant threw the three silver kopeks into the measure, shook the measure three times and lo! it was filled to the brim with silver kopeks! The Servant counted out the amount of the reckoning and handed the rest of the money to his master. Then he and Matti went on their way leaving the landlord gaping after them with open mouth.

Day after day the Servant paid the reckoning in the same way at the various inns where they stopped until they reached at last Matti's native village and the old house that still belonged to him.

They settled themselves there and one day the Servant said to Matti:

"Now, master, you know your fate: for having left your native village you know you are destined to marry a horned woman. You might as well do it at once for you'll have to do it sooner or later."

"That is true," Mattie said, "and if I knew the whereabouts of the horned woman who is my fate I should marry her at once."

"In that case we'll lose no more time," the Servant said. "The King has three daughters all of whom are horned. This isn't generally known but it is true. Let us go to the palace and present your suit. The King will give friendly ear for there are not many suitors for daughters with horns. He will try to make you take the oldest who has big horns and a hoarse voice. When she sees you, she'll whisper: 'Take me! Take me!' But do you shake your head and answer: 'No! Not this one!' Then the King will send for his second daughter. Her horns are not so big nor is her voice so hoarse. She, too, will whisper you: 'Take me! Take me!' But do you again shake your head and answer: 'No! Not this one!' Be firm and the King will finally have to send for his youngest daughter. Her horns are just soft little baby horns and her voice is just a little husky. Take her and soon all will be well."

So Matti and the Servant went to the palace and got audience with the King.

"My master, Matti," the Servant said, addressing the King, "is desirous of marrying a wife with horns."

The King was interested at once.

"As it happens I have a daughter with horns," he said. "I'll have her come in."

He sent for his oldest daughter and presently she appeared. Her horns were long and thick.

"Take me! Take me!" she whispered hoarsely as she passed Matti.

"See what a fine girl she is!" the King said, "and what well grown horns she has!"

But Matti shook his head.

"No, Your Majesty, I don't think I want to marry this one."

"Of course you must follow the dictates of your heart," the King said drily. "However, come to think of it, my second daughter also has horns. Maybe you'd like to consider her."

So the second daughter was called in. Her horns were not so large as her sister's nor was her voice so hoarse. But Matti, remembering the Servant's warning, refused her, too. The King seemed surprised and even annoyed that Matti should refuse his daughters so glibly, but when he found that Matti was firm he said:

"I have got another daughter, my youngest, but, if it's horns you're looking for, I don't believe you'll be interested in her at all since her horns are so small and soft that they are hardly noticeable at all. However, as you're here, you might as well see her."

So the youngest princess was sent for and at once Matti knew that she was the one he wanted to marry.

"She is under an evil enchantment and I am delivering her!"

She wasn't as beautiful as a princess should be but she was gentle and modest and when she passed Matti her cheeks flushed and she wasn't able to whisper anything. But Matti felt very sure that if she had whispered her voice would have been scarcely husky.

"This, O King," he said, "is my choice! Let me marry your youngest daughter and I promise to be a faithful husband to her."

The King would have preferred to marry off the older princesses first for their horns were getting to be very troublesome, but as they all had horns he was afraid to refuse Matti's offer.

So after a little talk he gave Matti the youngest and in a short time they were married.

After the wedding feast the King led the young couple to the bridal chamber and closed the door.

Matti's Servant meantime had gone out to the woods and cut some stout switches of birch. When the palace was quiet and all were asleep, he crept softly into the bridal chamber and, dragging the bride out of bed, he beat her unmercifully.

"Oh! Oh!" she cried in pain.

Her screams woke Matti and in fright he jumped out of bed and tried to stop the Servant.

"Wait!" the Servant said. "She is under an evil enchantment and I am delivering her!"

So he kept on beating her until he had drawn blood. Then instantly the horns fell from her head and there she stood a beautiful young girl released from the evil enchantment that had disfigured her.

The Servant handed her over to her husband who fell in love with her on sight and has loved her ever since.

"Now farewell, Matti," the Servant said. "My work is done and you will need me no longer. You have married a beautiful princess and the King will soon make you his heir."

With these words the Servant disappeared and Matti was left alone with his lovely bride.

And that was Matti's reward for having respected the dead. God Himself in the form of the Servant had come down and taken care of him.

FAMILIAR FACES

    I *Mary, Mary, So Contrary!*
   II *Jane, Jane, Don't Complain!*
  III *Susan Walker, What a Talker!*

When she got to the middle of the stream

I

MARY, MARY, SO CONTRARY!

There was once a farmer who was married to the most contrary wife in the world. Her name was Maya. If he expected Maya to say, "Yes," she would always say, "No," and if he expected her to say, "No," she would always say, "Yes." If he said the soup was too hot, Maya would instantly insist that it was too cold. She would do nothing that he wanted her to do, and she always insisted on doing everything that he did not want her to do.

Like most contrary people Maya was really very stupid and the farmer after he had been married to her for a few years knew exactly how to manage her.

For instance at Christmas one year he wanted to make a big feast for his friends and neighbors. Did he tell his wife so? Not he! Instead, a few weeks beforehand he remarked casually:

"Christmas is coming and I suppose every one will

expect us to have fine white bread. But I don't think we ought to. It's too expensive. Black bread is good enough for us."

"Black bread, indeed!" cried Maya. "Not at all! We're going to have white bread and you needn't say any more about it! Black bread at Christmas! To hear you talk people would suppose we are beggars!"

The farmer pretended to be grieved and he said:

"Well, my dear, have white bread if your heart is set on it, but I hope you don't expect to make any pies."

"Not make any pies! Just let me tell you I expect to make all the pies I want!"

"Well, now, Maya, if we have pies I don't think we ought to have any wine."

"No wine! I like that! Of course we'll have wine on Christmas!"

The farmer was much pleased but, still pretending to protest, he said:

"Well, if we spend money on wine, we better not expect to buy any coffee."

"What! No coffee on Christmas! Who ever heard of such a thing! Of course we'll have coffee!"

"Well, I'm not going to quarrel with you! Get a little coffee if you like, but just enough for you and me for I don't think we ought to have any guests."

"What! No guests on Christmas! Indeed and you're wrong if you think we're not going to have a houseful of guests!"

The farmer was overjoyed but, still pretending to grumble, he said:

"If you have the house full of people, you needn't think I'm going to sit at the head of the table, for I'm not!"

"You are, too!" screamed his wife. "That's exactly where you are going to sit!"

"Maya, Maya, don't get so excited! I will sit there if you insist. But if I do you mustn't expect me to pour the wine."

"And why not? It would be a strange thing if you didn't pour the wine at your own table!"

"All right, all right, I'll pour it! But you mustn't expect me to taste it beforehand."

"Of course you're going to taste it beforehand!"

This was exactly what the farmer wanted his wife to say. So you see by pretending to oppose her at every turn he was able to have the big Christmas party that he wanted and he was able to feast to his heart's content with all his friends and relatives and neighbors.

Time went by and Maya grew more and more contrary if such a thing were possible. Summer came and the haymaking season. They were going to a distant meadow to toss hay and had to cross an angry little river on a footbridge made of one slender plank.

The farmer crossed in safety, then he called back to his wife:

"Walk very carefully, Maya, for the plank is not strong!"

"I will not walk carefully!" the wife declared.

She flung herself on the plank with all her weight and when she got to the middle of the stream she jumped up and down just to show her husband how contrary she could be. Well, the plank broke with a snap, Maya fell into the water, the current carried her off, and she was drowned!

Her husband, seeing what had happened, ran madly upstream shouting:

"Help! Help!"

The haymakers heard him and came running to see what was the matter.

"My wife has fallen into the river!" he cried, "and the current has carried her body away!"

"What ails you?" the haymakers said. "Are you mad? If the current has carried your wife away, she's floating downstream, not upstream!"

"Any other woman would float downstream," the

farmer said. "Yes! But you know Maya! She's so contrary she'd float upstream every time!"

"That's true," the haymakers said, "she would!"

So all afternoon the farmer searched upstream for his wife's body but he never found it.

When night came he went home and had a good supper of all the things he liked to eat which Maya would never let him have.

They were so busy eating and drinking

II

JANE, JANE, DON'T COMPLAIN!

There was once a man who was poor and lazy and he had a wife who was even worse. Her name was Jenny. Jenny was so lazy that it was an effort for her to lift one foot after the other. And in addition to her laziness she was an everlasting complainer. "Oh!" she used to grunt in the morning, "I wish we didn't have to get up!" and "Oh!" she used to groan at night, "I wish we didn't have to take our shoes off before going to bed!"

One day when they were both out in the forest collecting faggots, Jenny said:

"I don't see why we're not rich! I don't see why the King should live at his ease while we have to grub for everything we get! I just hate work!"

Of course the trouble both with Jenny and her husband was not that they worked but that they didn't work. It was because they didn't that they had so much time to think about it.

"Drat it all!" Jenny went on, whining, "Adam and Eve are to blame for all our misfortunes! If they hadn't disobeyed God's commandment and eaten that apple, we'd all be living in the Garden of Eden to this day! It's all their fault that we have to moil and toil and hurry and scurry!"

"Yes," the man agreed, "it is, especially Eve's. Of course Adam was to blame, too, for he should have controlled his wife better. But Eve was the more to blame. If I had been Adam I shouldn't have allowed her to touch the apple in the first place."

Now it happened that the King who was out hunting that day overheard this conversation.

"Ha!" he thought to himself, "I've a great mind to teach these two people a lesson!"

He pushed aside the bushes that had hidden him from them and said:

"Good day to you both! I have just heard your complaints and I, too, think it very hard that you should be poor while others are rich. I tell you what I'll do: I'll take you both home with me to the castle and maintain you in ease and luxury provided you obey me in just one thing."

Jenny and her husband agreed to this eagerly and just as they were the King took them home with him to the castle. He lodged them in a room with golden furniture, he gave them fine clothes to wear, and for food he had them served the choicest delicacies in the world.

As they sat eating their first royal meal, he came in to them carrying in his hands a covered dish of silver. He put the dish down in the center of the table.

"Now, my friends," he said, "I promised to maintain you in this ease and luxury provided you obeyed me in one thing. You see this silver dish. I forbid you ever to lift the cover. If you disobey me, that moment I shall take from you your fine clothes and send you back to your poverty and misery."

With that the King left them and they stuffed themselves to their hearts' content with the delicate foods set before them.

They were so busy, eating and drinking and admiring themselves in their fine clothes, that for the first day they didn't give the covered dish a thought. The second day the wife noticed it and said:

"That's the thing we're not to touch. Well, for my part I don't want to touch it. I don't want to do anything but eat and sleep and try on my pretty new clothes."

By the third day they had eaten so much and so

steadily that they were no longer hungry and when they lay down on the big soft bed they no longer fell instantly asleep.

"Dear me," Jenny began whining, "I don't know what's the matter with this food! It doesn't taste as good as it used to! Maybe the cook has grown careless! I think we ought to complain to the King. I'm beginning to feel very uncomfortable and I haven't any appetite at all! I wonder what's in that covered dish. Perhaps it's something to eat, something perfectly delicious! I've half a mind to lift the cover and see."

"Now just you leave that silver dish alone!" the man growled. He, too, had been eating too much and was feeling peevish. "Don't you remember what the King said?"

"Pooh!" cried Jenny. "What do I care what the King said! I think he was just poking fun at us telling us we mustn't lift the cover of that silver dish. After all a dish is a dish and it's no crime to lift a cover even if it is made of silver!"

With that Jenny jumped up and before her husband could stop her she lifted the forbidden cover. Instantly a little white mouse hopped out of the silver dish and scurried away.

"Oh!" Jenny screamed, dropping the cover with a great clatter.

The King who was in an adjoining chamber heard the noise and came in.

"So!" he said, "you have done the one thing that I told you not to do! You haven't been here three days and although you've had everything that heart could wish for yet you couldn't obey me in this one little matter!"

"Your Majesty," the man said, "it was my wife who did it, not I."

"No matter," the King said, "you, too, are to blame. If you had restrained her it wouldn't have happened."

Then he called his servants and had them strip off the fine clothes and dress the couple again in their old rags.

"Now," he said as he drove them from the castle gates, "never again blame Adam and Eve for the misfortunes which you bring upon yourselves!"

They carried home the treasure on their backs

III

SUSAN WALKER, WHAT A TALKER!

There was once a man whose wife was an awful talker. Her name was Susanna. No matter how important it was to keep a matter quiet, if Susanna knew about it, she just had to talk. She was always running to the neighbors and exclaiming:

"Oh, my dear, have you heard so and so?"

Her husband was an industrious fellow. He set nets in the river, he snared birds in the forest, and he worked at any odd jobs that came along.

It happened one day while he was out in the forest that he found a buried treasure.

"Ah!" he thought to himself, "now I can buy a little farm that will keep me and Susanna comfortable the rest of our days!"

He started home at once to tell his wife the good fortune that had befallen them. He had almost reached home when he stopped, suddenly realizing that the first thing Susanna would do would be to spread the news broadcast throughout the village. Then of course the government would get wind of his find and presently officers of the law would come and confiscate the entire treasure.

"That would never do," he told himself. "I must think out some plan whereby I can let Susanna know about the treasure without risking the loss of it."

He puzzled over the matter for a long time and at last hit upon something that he thought might prove successful.

In his nets that day he had caught a pike and in one of his snares he had found a grouse. He went back now to the river and put the bird in the fishnet, and then he went to the woods and put the fish in the snare. This done he went home and at once told Susanna about the buried treasure which was going to be the means of making their old age comfortable.

She flew at once into great excitement.

"La! La! A buried treasure! Whoever heard of such luck! Oh, how all the neighbors will envy us when they hear about it! I can hardly wait to tell them!"

"But they mustn't hear!" her husband told her. "You don't want the officers of the law coming and taking it all from us, do you?"

"That would be a nice how-do-you-do!" Susanna cried. "What! Come and take our treasure that you found yourself in the forest?"

"Yes, my dear, that's exactly what they'd do if once they heard about it."

"Well, you can depend upon it, my dear husband, not a soul will hear about it from me!"

She shook her head vigorously and repeated this many times and then tried to slip out of the house on some such excuse as needing to borrow a cup of meal from a neighbor.

But the man insisted on her staying beside him all evening. She kept remembering little errands that would take her to the houses of various neighbors but each time she attempted to leave her husband called her back. At last he got her safely to bed.

Early next morning, before she had been able to talk to any one, he said:

"Now, my dear, come with me to the forest and help me to carry home the treasure. On the way we'd better see if we've got anything in the nets and the snares."

They went first to the river and when the man had lifted his nets they found a grouse which he made Susanna reach over and get. Then in the woods he let her make the discovery of a pike in one of the snares.

She was all the while so excited about the treasure that she hadn't mind enough left to be surprised that a bird should be caught in a fishnet and a fish in a birdsnare.

Well, they found the precious treasure and they stowed it away in two sacks which they carried home on their backs. On the way home Susanna could scarcely refrain from calling out to every passerby some hint of their good fortune. As they passed the house of Helmi, her dearest crony, she said to her husband:

"My dear, won't you just wait here a moment while I run in and get a drink of water?"

"You mustn't go in just now," her husband said. "Don't you hear what's going on?"

There was the sound of two dogs fighting and yelping in the kitchen.

"Helmi is getting a beating from her husband," the man said. "Can't you hear her crying? This is no time for an outsider to appear."

All that day and all that night he kept so close to Susanna that the poor woman wasn't able to exchange a word with another human being.

Early next morning she escaped him and ran as fast as her legs could carry her to Helmi's house.

"My dear," she began all out of breath, "such a

wonderful treasure as we've found but I've sworn never to whisper a word about it for fear the government should hear of it! I should have stopped and told you yesterday but your husband was beating you—"

"What's that?" cried Helmi's husband who came in just then and caught the last words.

"It's the treasure we've found!"

"The treasure? What are you talking about? Begin at the beginning."

"Well, my old man and me we started out yesterday morning and first we went to the river to see if there was anything in the nets. We found a grouse—"

"A grouse?"

"Yes, we found a grouse in the nets. Then we went to the forest and looked in the snares and in one we found a pike."

"A pike!"

"Yes. Then we went and dug up the treasure and put it in two sacks and you could have seen us yourself carrying it home on our backs but you were too busy beating poor Helmi."

"I beating poor Helmi! Ho! Ho! Ho! That is a good one! I was busy beating my wife while you were getting birds out of fishnets and fish out of snares! Ho! Ho! Ho!"

"It's so!" Susanna cried. "It is so! You were so beating Helmi! And you sounded just like two dogs fighting! And we did so carry home the treasure!"

But Helmi's husband only laughed the harder. That afternoon when he went to the Inn he was still laughing and when the men there asked him what was so funny he told them Susanna's story and soon the whole village was laughing at the foolish woman who found birds in fishnets and fish in snares and who thought that two yelping dogs were Helmi and her husband fighting.

As for the treasure that wasn't taken any more seriously than the grouse and the pike.

"It must have been two sacks of turnips they carried home on their backs!" the village people decided.

The husband of course said nothing and Susanna, too, was soon forced to keep quiet for now whenever she tried to explain people only laughed.

MIKKO, THE FOX

A Nursery Epic in Sixteen Adventures

Osmo, the Bear, grunted out: "Huh! That's easy! We'll eat the smallest of us next!"

ADVENTURE I

THE ANIMALS TAKE A BITE

 A Farmer once dug a pit to trap the Animals that had been stealing his grain. By a strange chance he fell into his own pit and was killed.

The Ermine found him there.

"H'm," thought the Ermine, "that's the Farmer himself, isn't it? I better take him before any one else gets him."

So the Ermine dragged the Farmer's body out of the pit, put it on a sledge, and then, after taking a bite, began hauling it away.

Presently he met the Squirrel who clapped his hands in surprise.

"God bless you, brother!" the Squirrel exclaimed, "what's that you're hauling behind you?"

"It's the Farmer himself," the Ermine explained. "He fell into the pit that he had digged for us poor forest folk and serve him right, too! Take a bite of him and then come along and help me pull."

"Very well," the Squirrel said.

He took a bite of the Farmer and then marched along beside the Ermine, helping him to pull the sledge.

Presently they met Jussi, the Hare. Jussi looked at then in amazement, his eyes popping out of his head.

"Mercy me!" he cried, "what's that you two are hauling?"

"It's the Farmer," the Ermine explained. "He fell into the pit that he digged for us poor forest folk and serve him right, too! Take a bite of him, Jussi, and then come along and help us pull."

So Jussi, the Hare, took a bite of the Farmer and then marched along beside the Ermine and the Squirrel helping them to pull the sledge.

Next they met Mikko, the Fox.

"Goodness me!" Mikko said, "what's that you three are hauling?"

The Ermine again explained:

"It's the Farmer. He fell into the pit that he had digged for us poor forest folk and serve him right, too! Take a bite of him, Mikko, and then come along and help us pull."

So Mikko, the Fox, took a bite and then marched along beside the Ermine and the Squirrel and the Hare helping them to pull the sledge.

Next they met Pekka, the Wolf.

"Good gracious!" Pekka cried, "what's that you four are hauling?"

The Ermine explained:

"It's the Farmer. He fell into the pit that he had digged for us poor forest folk and serve him right, too! Take a bite of him, Pekka, and then help us pull."

So Pekka, the Wolf, took a bite and then marched along beside the Ermine, the Squirrel, the Hare, and the Fox, helping them to pull the sledge.

Next they met Osmo, the Bear.

"Good heavens!" Osmo rumbled, "what's that you five are hauling?"

"It's the Farmer," the Ermine explained. "He fell into the pit that he had digged for us poor forest folk and serve him right, too! Take a bite of him, Osmo, and then help us pull."

So Osmo, the Bear, took a bite and then marched along beside the Ermine, the Squirrel, the Hare, the Fox, and the Wolf, helping them to pull the sledge.

Well, they pulled and they pulled and whenever they felt tired or hungry they stopped and took a bite until the Farmer was about finished.

Then Pekka, the Wolf, said:

"See here, brothers, we've eaten up every bit of the Farmer except his beard. What are we going to eat now?"

Osmo, the Bear, grunted out:

"Huh! That's easy! We'll eat the smallest of us next!"

He had no sooner spoken than the Squirrel ran up a tree and the Ermine slipped under a stone.

Pekka, the Wolf said:

"But the smallest have escaped!"

Osmo, the Bear, grunted again:

"Huh! The smallest now is that pop-eyed Jussi! Let's—"

At mention of his name the Hare went loping across the field and was soon at a safe distance.

Osmo, the Bear, put his heavy paw on the Fox's shoulder.

"Mikko," he said, "it's your turn now for you're the smallest of us three."

Mikko, the Fox, pretended not to be at all afraid.

"That's true," he said, "I'm the smallest. All right, brothers, I'm ready. But before you eat me I wish you'd take me to the top of the hill. Down here in the valley it's so gloomy."

"Very well," the others agreed, "we'll go where you say. It is more cheerful there."

As they climbed the hill the Fox whispered to the Wolf:

"Sst! Pekka! When you eat me whose turn will it be then? Who will be the smallest then?"

"Mercy me!" the Wolf cried, "it will be my turn then, won't it?"

The terror of the thought quite took his appetite away.

"See here, Osmo," he said to the Bear, "I don't think it would be right for us to eat Mikko. You and I and Mikko ought to be friends and live together in peace. Now let's take a vote on the matter and we'll do whatever the majority says. I vote that we three be friends. What do you say, Mikko?"

The Fox said that he agreed with the Wolf. It

would be much better all around if they three were friends.

"Well," grunted Osmo, the Bear, "it's no use my voting for you two make a majority. But I must say I'm sorry to have you vote this way for I'm hungry."

So the three animals, the Bear, the Wolf, and the Fox, agreed henceforward to be friends and planned to live near each other in the woods behind the Farm.

ADVENTURE II

THE PARTNERS

 The Bear and the Wolf and the Fox made houses quite close together and the Wolf and the Fox decided to go into partnership.

"The first thing we ought to do," said Pekka, the Wolf, "is make a clearing in the forest and plant some crops."

The Fox agreed and the very next day they started out to work. Each had a crock with three pats of butter for his dinner. They left their crocks in the cool water of a little spring in the forest not far from the place where they had decided to make a clearing.

It was hard work felling trees and the Fox, soon tiring of it, made some sort of excuse to run off. When he came back he said to the Wolf:

"Pekka, the folks at the Farm are having a christening and have sent me an invitation to attend."

"It's too bad we're so busy to-day," the Wolf said. "Another day you might have gone."

"But I must go," the Fox insisted. "They've been good neighbors to us and they'd be insulted if I refused."

"Very well," the Wolf said, "if you feel that way about it you better go. But hurry back for we have a lot to do."

So the Fox trotted off but he got no farther than the spring where the butter crocks were cooling. He took the Wolf's crock and licked off the top layer of butter. Then after a while he went back to the clearing.

"Well, Mikko," the Wolf said, "is the christening over?"

"Yes, it's over."

"What did they name the child?"

"They named it Top."

"Top? That's a strange name!"

In a few moments the Fox again ran off and returned

with the announcement that there was to be another christening at the Farm and again they wanted him to attend.

"Another christening!" the Wolf exclaimed. "How can that be?"

"This time the daughter has a baby."

"You're not going, are you, Mikko? You can't always be going to christenings."

"That's true, Pekka, that's true," said the Fox, "but I think I must go this time."

The Wolf sighed.

"You will hurry back, won't you? This work is too much for me alone."

"Yes, Pekka dear," the Fox promised, "I'll hurry back as quickly as I can."

So he trotted off again to the spring and the Wolf's butter crock. This time he ate the middle pat of the Wolf's butter, then slowly sauntered back to the clearing.

"Well," said the Wolf, pausing a moment in his work, "what did they name the baby this time?"

"This one they named Middle."

"Middle? That's a strange name to give a baby!"

For a few moments the Fox pretended to work hard. Then he ran off again. When he came back, he said:

"Pekka, do you know they're having another christening at the Farm and they say that I just must come."

"Another christening! Now, Mikko, that's too much! How can they be having another christening?"

"Well, this time it's the daughter-in-law that has a baby."

"I don't care who it is," the Wolf said, "you just can't go. You've got some work to do, you have!"

The Fox agreed:

"You're right, Pekka, you're right! I'm entirely too busy to be running off all the time to christenings! I'd say, 'No!' in a minute if it wasn't that we are new settlers and they are our nearest neighbors. As it is I'm afraid they'd think it wasn't neighborly if I didn't come. But I'll hurry back, I promise you!"

So for the third time the Fox trotted off to the little spring and this time he licked the Wolf's butter crock clean to the bottom. Then he went slowly back to the clearing and told the Wolf about the christening and the baby.

"They've named this one Bottom," he said.

"Bottom!" the Wolf echoed. "What funny names they give children nowadays!"

The Fox pretended to work hard for a few minutes, then threw himself down exhausted.

"*Wake up, Pekka!*
Wake up! There's
butter running out of your nose!"

"Heigh ho!" he said, with a yawn, "I'm so tired and hungry it must be dinner time!"

The Wolf looked at the sun and said:

"Yes, I think we had better rest now and eat."

So they went to the spring and got their butter crocks. The Wolf found that his had already been licked clean.

"Mikko!" he cried, "have you been at my butter?"

"Me?" the Fox said in a tone of great innocence. "How could I have been at your butter when you know perfectly well that I've been working right beside you all morning except when I was away at the christenings? You must have eaten up your butter yourself!"

"Of course I haven't eaten it up myself!" the Wolf declared. "I just bet anything you took it!"

The Fox pretended to be much aggrieved.

"Pekka, I won't have you saying such a thing! We must get at the bottom of this! I tell you what we'll do: we'll both lie down in the sun and the heat of the sun will melt the butter and make it run. Now then, if butter runs out of my nose then I'm the one that has eaten your butter; if it runs out of your nose, then you've eaten it yourself. Do you agree to this test?"

The Wolf said, yes, he agreed, and at once lay down in the sun. He had been working so hard that he was very tired and in a few moments he was sound asleep. Thereupon the Fox slipped over and daubed a little lump of butter on the end of his nose. The sun melted the butter and then, of course, it looked as if it were running out of the Wolf's nose.

"Wake up, Pekka! Wake up!" the Fox cried. "There's butter running out of your nose!"

The Wolf awoke and felt his nose with his tongue.

"Why, Mikko," he said in surprise, "so there is! Well, I suppose I must have eaten that butter myself but I give you my word for it I don't remember doing it!"

"Well," said the Fox, pretending still to feel hurt, "you shouldn't always suspect me."

When they went back to the clearing, the Wolf began pulling the brush together to burn it up and the Fox slipped away and lay down behind some brushes.

"Mikko! Mikko!" the Wolf called. "Aren't you going to help me burn the brush?"

"You set it a-fire," the Fox called back, "and I'll stay here to guard against any flying sparks. We don't want to burn down the whole forest!"

So the Wolf burned up all the brush while the Fox took a pleasant nap.

Then when he was ready to plant the seed in the rich wood ashes, the Wolf again called out to the Fox to come help him.

"You do the planting, Pekka," the Fox called back, "and I'll stay here and frighten off the birds. If I don't they'll come and pick up every seed you plant."

So Mikko, the rascal, took another nap while the poor Wolf planted the field he had already cleared and burned.

ADVENTURE III

THE FOX AND THE CROW

In a short time the field that Pekka, the Wolf, had planted began to sprout. Pekka was delighted.

"See, Mikko," he said to the Fox, "our grain is growing and we shall soon be harvesting it!"

The Fox turned up his nose indifferently.

"If we don't get something to eat before that grain ripens," he said, "we'll starve, both of us! While we wait for the harvest I think we better go out hunting. I'm going this minute for I tell you I'm hungry!"

The Fox went sniffing into the forest and finally came

to the tree where Harakka, the Magpie, had her nest. The Fox, cocking his head, paced slowly round and round the tree, looking at it from every angle. Harakka, the Magpie, sitting on her nest among her fledglings began to feel nervous.

"Say, Mikko," she called down, "what are you looking at?"

At first the Fox made no answer. Deep in thought, apparently, he nodded his head and murmured:

"Yes, the very tree!"

Harakka, the Magpie, again called down:

"What are you looking at, Mikko?"

The Fox started as though he had heard the question for the first time.

"Ah, Harakka, is that you? Good day to you! I hope you are well! I hope the children are all well! I was so busy looking for the right tree that I didn't recognize you at first. You see I have to cut down a tree to get wood for a new pair of *skis*. This tree is just the one I want."

"Oh, mercy me!" the Magpie cried. "You can't cut down this tree! Do you want to kill all my children? This is our home!"

Mikko, the rascal, pretended to be very sympathetic.

"I'm awfully sorry to have to disturb you, truly I am, but I'm afraid I do have to cut down this tree. I can't find another that suits me as well."

The Magpie flapped her wings in despair.

"You hard-hearted wretch! What will you take not to cut down this tree?"

The Fox put his paw to his head and pretended to think hard. After a moment he said:

"Well, Harakka, I'll make you this offer: I'll leave this tree standing provided you throw me down one of your fledglings."

"What!" the poor Magpie shrieked. "Give you one of my babies! I'll never do that! Never! Never! *Never!*"

"Oh, very well! Just as you like! If I cut the tree down I can get them all. But I thought for the sake of old times I'd ask for only one. However, do as you think best."

What could the poor Magpie say? If the tree were felled and her fledglings thrown out of the nest they would certainly all perish. Perhaps it would be wise to sacrifice one to save the rest.

"You promise to let the tree stand," she said, "if I give you one of my children?"

"Yes," the rascal promised, "just drop me one of your

fledglings, a nice plump one, and I won't cut down the tree."

With shaking claw Harakka pushed one of her children over the edge of the nest. It fluttered to the ground and Mikko carried it off.

Well, the next day what did that Fox do but come back and begin pacing around the tree again.

"Yes," he said, pretending to talk to himself, "this is the best tree I can find. I might as well cut it down at once."

"But, Mikko!" cried the Magpie, "you forget! You said you wouldn't cut down this tree if I gave you one of my children and I did give you one!"

The Fox flipped his tail indifferently.

"I know," he said, "I did promise but I thought then I could find another tree that would suit me as well as this one, but I can't. I've looked everywhere and I can't. I'm sorry but I'm afraid that I'll just have to take this tree."

"O dear, O dear, O dear!" the poor distracted Magpie wept. "Will nothing make you leave this tree stand?"

The Fox smacked his lips.

"Well, Harakka, drop me down another of your fledglings and I won't disturb the tree. I promise."

"What! Another of my babies! Oh, you wretch!"

"Well, suit yourself," Mikko said. "One of your fledglings and you can keep the others safe in the nest, or I'll cut the tree down."

What could the poor Magpie do? Wouldn't it be better to sacrifice another fledgling on the chance of saving the rest? Yes, it would! So she pushed another out of the nest. It fluttered to the ground and Mikko, the rascal, carried it off.

That afternoon Varis, the Crow, came to call on the Magpie.

"Why, my dear," she said, looking over the fledglings, "two of your children are missing! Whatever has become of them?"

"It's that rascally Mikko!" the Magpie cried, and thereupon she told her friend the whole story.

Varis, the Crow, listened carefully and then said:

"My dear, that miserable Fox has been fooling you! Why, he can't cut down this tree or any other tree for that matter! He hasn't even got an ax! Don't let him impose on you a third time!"

So the very next day when the Fox came and again tried the same little trick, Harakka, the Magpie, tossed her head scornfully and said:

"Go along, you rascal! You can't fool me again!

How can you cut down this tree or any other for that matter when you haven't even got an ax!"

The Fox was furious at being cheated of his dinner.

"You didn't think that out yourself, Harakka!" he said. "Some one's been talking to you! Who was it?"

"It was my dear friend, Varis," the Magpie said. "She's on to your tricks!"

"I'll teach that Crow to interfere with my affairs!" the Fox muttered to himself as he trotted off.

He went to an open field and lay down with his mouth open, pretending to be dead.

"I'm sure Varis will soon spy me!" he said to himself.

He was right. Presently the Crow began circling above him. She flew nearer and nearer and at last alighted on his head. His tongue was lolling out and Varis decided to have her first bite there. She gave it a sharp peck at which the Fox jumped up and caught her in his paws.

"Ha! Ha!" he cried. "So you're the one who spoiled my little game with Harakka, are you? Well, I'll teach you not to interfere with me! As I haven't got one of Harakka's fledglings for my dinner, I'm going to take you!"

"You don't mean you're going to eat me!" cried the Crow in terror.

"I'll teach that Crow to interfere with my affairs!" the Fox muttered to himself as he trotted off

"That's exactly what I mean!"

"No, no, Mikko! Don't do that!"

"Yes, that's exactly what I'm going to do! I'm going to teach you birds that I'm not an animal to be played jokes on!"

"I suppose," the Crow said, sighing, "if it must be, it must be! But, Mikko, if you really want to use me as a warning to the other birds, you oughtn't to eat me right down. It would be much better if you dragged me along the ground first. Then they'd see a wing here, a leg there, and a long trail of feathers. That really would terrify them."

"I believe you're right," the Fox said.

He put the Crow down on the ground and lifted his paw for a moment to change his hold. The Crow instantly jerked away and escaped.

"Ha! Ha!" she cawed as she flew off. "You were clever enough to catch me, Mikko, but you weren't clever enough to eat me when you had me!"

So this was one time when Mikko, the Fox, was worsted.

ADVENTURE IV

THE CHIEF MOURNER

"Mercy me!" thought Mikko to himself as he watched Varis, the Crow, fly away, "this is certainly my unlucky day! There I had my dinner right in my hand and then lost it!"

Sighing and shaking his head he sauntered slowly back to the forest.

Now it happened that Osmo, the Bear, had just lost his wife and was out looking for some one to bewail her death. The first person he met was Pekka, the Wolf.

"Pekka," he said, "my wife's dead and I'm out looking for a good strong mourner. Can you mourn?"

"Me? Indeed I can! Just listen!"

Pekka, the Wolf, pointed his nose to the sky and let out a long shivery howl.

"There!" he said. "I don't believe you'll find any one that can do any better than that!"

But Osmo, the Bear, shook his head.

"No, Pekka, you won't do. I don't like your mourning at all!"

The Bear ambled on and presently he met the Hare.

"Good day, Jussi," he said. "Are you any good at mourning? Show me what you can do."

The Hare gave some frightened squeaks as his idea of mourning the dead.

"No, no," Osmo said, "I don't like your mourning either."

So he walked on farther until by chance he met the Fox.

"Mikko," he said, "my wife's dead and I'm out looking for a good strong mourner. Can you mourn?"

"Can I? Indeed I can!" the Fox declared. "I'm a marvel at mourning! I can wail high and low and soft and loud and just any way you want! Listen!" And Mikko, beginning with a little whimpering sound,

And Mikko, beginning with a little whimpering sound, slowly rose to a high heart-rending cry

slowly rose to a high heartrending cry. This is what he wailed:

> "*Med! Med! Med!*
> The Bear's Wife is dead!
> *Lax! Lax! Lax!*
> No more she'll spin the flax!
> *Eyes! Eyes! Eyes!*
> No more she'll bake the pies!
> *Air! Air! Air!*
> No more she'll drive the mare!
> *Shakes! Shakes! Shakes!*
> There'll be no more little cakes!
> *Darth! Darth! Darth!*
> Throw the pots on the hearth
> For the Bear's Wife is dead!
> *Med! Med! Med!*"

Osmo, the Bear, was deeply moved.

"Beautiful! Beautiful!" he grunted hoarsely. "How well you knew her! Come along home with me, Mikko, and start right in! Oh, how beautifully you wail!"

So Mikko went home with the Bear. The old Bear Wife was laid out on a bench in the kitchen.

"Now then," the Bear said, "you begin the wailing while I cook the porridge."

"No, no, Osmo," the Fox said, "I couldn't possibly wail in here! The place is full of smoke and my voice would get husky in two minutes! Can't you lay her out in the storehouse?"

The Bear demurred but the Fox insisted and at last had his way. So together they dragged the body of the old Bear Wife out to the storehouse. The Fox stood beside the body ready to begin his wailing and the Bear went back to the kitchen.

The moment the Bear was out of sight Mikko, the rascal, instead of bewailing the old Bear Wife began gobbling her up! He just gobbled and gobbled and gobbled as fast as he could.

"What's the matter?" the Bear called out after a few minutes. "Why don't you begin?"

The Fox made no reply but kept on gobbling as hard as he could.

"Mikko! Mikko!" the Bear called out again. "What's the matter? Why aren't you howling?"

By this time the Fox had made a good dinner, so he called back:

"Don't bother me! I'm busy eating! Yum! Yum! Yum! Bear meat is awful good! Just give me a few more minutes and I'll be finished!"

At that the Bear rushed out of the kitchen in a terrible rage but the Fox was already running off and the Bear was unable to catch him. He did hit the end of his tail with the long spoon with which he had been measuring the meal, but that was all.

Mikko, the rascal, got safely away. However, to this day his tail shows the white mark of the meal.

ADVENTURE V

MIRRI, THE CAT

One day while the Fox was out walking in the forest he met a stranger.

"Good day," he said. "Who are you?"

"I am Mirri," the stranger said, "a poor unfortunate Cat out of employment. I had service in a decent family but I've had to leave them."

"Did they treat you badly?" the Fox asked.

"No, it wasn't that. They were considerate enough but they kept getting poorer and poorer until finally they hadn't food enough to feed us animals. Then I overheard the master say that soon they'd be forced to eat us and that they'd begin with me. At that I decided it was time for me to run away and here I am."

"My poor Cat," Mikko said, "you've had a cruel experience! Why don't you take service with me?"

"Will I be safe with you?" the Cat asked. "Will you protect me?"

"Will I?" the Fox repeated boastfully. "My dear Mirri, once it becomes known that you are Mikko's servant all the animals will show you a wholesome respect."

"Well then, I'll enter your service," the Cat said.

So the bargain was struck and the Fox at once began to train his new servant.

"Now, Mirri, tell me: what would you do if you suddenly met a Bear?"

"There's just one thing I could do, master: I'd run up a tree."

The Fox laughed.

"You must have more ways than one to meet such a situation! Take me now: there are any of a hundred things that I could do if I met a Bear!"

Just then Osmo, the Bear, ambled softly up behind the Fox. The Cat saw him and instantly flew up a

He jerked quickly away and fled and the Bear was left standing with his mouth wide open

tree. Before the Fox could move Osmo clutched him firmly on the shoulder with his teeth.

"Oh, master, master!" the Cat called down from the tree. "What's this? I with my one way have escaped and you with your hundred are caught!"

But the Fox paid no heed to the Cat. He twisted his head around and looked reproachfully at the Bear.

"Why, Osmo, my dear old friend!" he said, "what in the world do you mean taking hold of me so roughly! Ouch! You're nipping my shoulder, really you are! I don't understand why you're acting this way! Here I've always been such a good friend to you, so faithful, so true, so—"

"What!" rumbled the Bear. "Faithful! True! Oh, you—"

Osmo's feelings overcame him to such an extent that he opened his jaws to roar out freely his denial of the Fox's hypocrisy.

That gave the Fox just the chance he wanted. He jerked quickly away and fled and the Bear was left standing with his mouth wide open.

Later when the Bear had ambled off the Fox returned and called the Cat down from the tree.

"You see, Mirri," he remarked casually, "it wasn't anything at all for me to get the best of the Bear!"

He could see that he had vastly impressed the Cat, so he let the subject drop.

"Come along, Mirri," he said, "it's time for us to go home."

A terrible creature landed on his nose and drove it full of pins and needles

ADVENTURE VI

THE FOX'S SERVANT

A day or so later the Fox met Pekka, the Wolf. The Fox hadn't seen much of Pekka recently for Pekka had been having a hard time and had been on the verge of starvation. Now he was sleek again and well fed for he had recently killed an Ox.

"Good day, Pekka," the Fox said in a friendly way.

"Good day, Mikko. How are you?"

"Very fine indeed!" the Fox said. "You see I have a new servant. Oh, he's a wonderful servant! He's not big to look at, you know, but he's so strong and quick that he'd jump on you in a minute and eat you up before you knew what was happening!"

"Really, Mikko?"

"Yes, really! You just ought to see him!"

"I'd like to see him," the Wolf said.

"Well, you might slip down now and take a peep in the kitchen. He's at home. But, my dear Pekka, I warn you not to let him see you! If he catches sight of you, I won't be responsible for the consequences!"

The Wolf was deeply impressed with all this. He crept carefully down to the Fox's kitchen and sniffed cautiously at the crack under the door. The Cat inside, seeing the tip of the Wolf's nose and thinking it was a Mouse, pounced on it with all his claws. This gave the Wolf a mighty fright and he bolted madly off into the forest.

He was still panting when he met the Bear.

"Osmo," he said, "have you heard about that awful creature that Mikko has for a servant?"

The Bear had heard nothing, so the Wolf related to him his own terrifying experience.

The Bear's curiosity was aroused.

"I must have a glimpse of this wonderful servant," he said, ambling off in the direction of the Fox's kitchen.

"I'll wait for you here," the Wolf called after him, "and I warn you, Osmo, be careful!"

The Bear when he got to the Fox's kitchen quietly stuck his nose under the crack of the door and squinted inside. He hardly had time for one squint when a terrible creature with a straight tail that looked like a spear came flying through the air, landed on his nose, and drove it full of pins and needles.

"Ouch! Ouch! Ouch!" the Bear whimpered as he hurried back to the Wolf.

"Did you see him?" the Wolf asked.

"I got just one glimpse of him," the Bear said. "He had a long spear sticking up over his shoulder and he came swooping down through the air just as if he had wings!"

"My! I wish we could really see him!" the Wolf said. "Suppose we ask Mikko to arrange some way we can have a good look at him."

So they went to the Fox and Mikko, the rascal, said:

"Well, now, if you make a feast and invite my servant I think he will come."

"All right," the Wolf said, "that's what we'll do. I've still got some of that ox. It will make a fine feast."

So they roasted the remains of the ox and set it out.

"Now I'll go get my servant," the Fox said. "When

you hear us coming, you two hide some place where you can see us but we can't see you. If my servant once sees you I won't be responsible for the consequences!"

So the Wolf hid in some bushes nearby and the Bear drew himself up into the branches of a tree.

Well, the Fox and the Cat arrived and sat them down to the feast. Now it happened that the Wolf was not able to see, so he tried to twist himself around into a better position. The Cat caught a glimpse of his tail moving in the bushes and instantly pounced on it. With one terrified yelp, the Wolf jumped out of the bushes and fled into the forest as fast as he could.

In fright the Cat scampered up the tree and the Bear, of course, supposed that the awful creature now was after him. In his frantic efforts to escape he tumbled down out of the tree and broke two ribs. But for all that he made off, too terrified to look back.

So the Fox and the Cat were left to finish the ox in peace.

ADVENTURE VII

THE WOLF SINGS

 Having sacrificed his ox in order to feast the Fox's servant, the Wolf had nothing left for himself and was soon very hungry. He could find nothing to eat in the forest, so he went prowling around a farm in hopes of getting a pig or a chicken. The only living creature he came upon was a thin old Dog asleep in the sun.

"This is better than nothing," he thought to himself and, taking hold of the Dog, he began dragging it off.

"Cousin! Cousin!" cried the Dog. "Is this any way to treat a relation? Let me go!"

"I'm sorry," the Wolf said, "but I can't let you go. I'm too hungry."

"Let me go," the Dog begged, "and I tell you what I'll do: I'll give you a bottle of vodka."

"Promises come easy," the Wolf said. "Where will you get the vodka?"

"Under the bench in the kitchen. That's where the master keeps his bottle. I've seen him hide it there. Come to-night after the family's asleep and I'll let you in and give you the vodka."

Now Pekka, the Wolf, was very fond of vodka, so he said to the Dog:

"Very well, I'll let you go. But see that you keep your promise!"

Late that night when the family were asleep, the Wolf came scratching at the farmhouse door and the Dog let him in.

"Well, old fellow, you know why I've come," the Wolf said.

At once the Dog crawled under the bench and got the master's bottle of vodka.

"Here, Pekka, here it is!" he said, offering the Wolf the bottle.

The Wolf went staggering around the room howling at the top of his voice

"You drink first," Pekka insisted. "You're the host."

The Dog raised the bottle and took a little sip. Then the Wolf took a deep swallow.

"Ah!" he said, smacking his lips, "that's something like!"

His stomach was empty and the vodka went through his veins like fire. He felt happy and laughed and went capering around the room.

"I feel like singing!" he cried.

"My dear Pekka," the Dog said, "I beg you don't sing! You will wake the folks! Sit down quietly and we'll talk."

So they sat awhile and talked and then the Wolf took another deep swallow of the vodka. Again he wanted to sing and the Dog had trouble in restraining him.

"Do you want to wake the family, Pekka? Be quiet now or you can't have any more vodka!"

The Wolf took another deep drink and after that there was no holding him back. He went staggering around the room howling at the top of his voice.

The Farmer and all his family came hurrying into the kitchen with clubs and pokers and whatever they could pick up.

"It's a Wolf!" the Farmer cried. "The impudent scoundrel, coming right into the house! Give him a good beating!"

If the door hadn't been open they would have clubbed poor Pekka to death. As it was he barely escaped with his life.

In the confusion that followed the Wolves stampeded, running helter-skelter in all directions

ADVENTURE VIII

THE CLEVER GOAT

The truth is Pekka, the Wolf, was a pretty stupid fellow always getting into some scrape or other. With sore ribs and a back aching from the beating which the farm folk had given him he slunk quietly along the forest ways hoping to come upon some easy prey. Suddenly he saw ahead of him a Goat and a Ram.

"What are they doing hereabouts?" he thought to himself. "This is no place for them and if anything happens to them it will be their own fault."

Vuhi, the Goat, and Dinas, the Ram, both knew that the forest was no place for them. But where else could they go? They had recently been turned loose to fend for themselves by their poor old master who was no longer able to feed them.

"This forest rather frightens me," the Ram had said to the Goat. "Do you suppose we'll be able to keep off the Wolves?"

Vuhi, the Goat, flirted his whiskers and said:

"I've got a plan."

Thereupon he took a sack and half filled it with dry chips. Then when he shook the sack the chips made a hollow rattle. He threw the sack over his shoulder and said to the Ram:

"Don't you be frightened, Dinas. We'll be able to hold our own with the forest creatures."

It was just at this moment that Pekka, the Wolf, appeared.

"Ha! Ha!" said Pekka suspiciously. "What's that you've got in that sack? No nonsense now! Answer me at once or I'll have to kill you both!"

Vuhi, the Goat, gave the sack a little rattle.

"In this sack?" he said. "Oh, only the skulls and bones of the Wolves we have eaten. We haven't had any Wolf meat now for some time, have we, Dinas? It's good you've come along for we're hungry. . . . Attention, Dinas! Kill the Wolf!"

The Ram lowered his horns ready for attack and Pekka, the Wolf, too surprised to resist and too stiff to run away, cried out wildly:

"Brothers! Brothers! Don't kill me! I'm your friend! Spare me and I'll do something for you!"

"Attention, Dinas!" the Goat commanded. "Don't kill the Wolf just yet!"

Then he asked Pekka:

"What will you do for us if we spare you?"

"I'll send you twelve Wolves," Pekka promised. "That will give you more meat than you'd have if you killed just me!"

"Twelve," the Goat replied. "You are right: twelve Wolves will give us more meat than one. Very well, we'll let you go on condition that you send us twelve. But see you keep your word!"

So the Wolf went off as fast as his stiff legs could carry him and assembled twelve of his brothers.

"I've called you together," he said, "to warn you of two terrible creatures, a Goat and a Ram, who are here in the forest eating up Wolves! Already they have a sack full of our unfortunate relations' skulls and bones! I saw the sack myself! Don't you think we ought all of us to flee?"

"What!" said the other Wolves, "thirteen Wolves turn tail on one Goat and one Ram? Never! We'll go together and give them battle!"

"Don't count me in!" Pekka said. "I don't want to see those two again!"

So the twelve Wolves marched off without Pekka.

The Goat as he saw them coming ran up a tree. The Ram followed him but couldn't get very high.

The twelve Wolves came under the tree and standing in close formation called out:

"Now then, you two, come on! We're ready for you!"

"Attention, Dinas!" the Goat commanded. "They're all here, so lose no more time! Jump down among them and kill them!"

The Goat himself began climbing down the tree, at the same time making an awful noise with his sack. He gave the Ram a push and the Ram slipped and fell right on the backs of the Wolves.

"That's right, Dinas! Kill them all!" the Goat shouted, rattling his sack more furiously than ever. "Don't let one of them escape!"

In the confusion that followed the Wolves stampeded, running helter-skelter in all directions. Every Wolf there felt that his own escape was a piece of rare good fortune.

"Those terrible two!" he thought.

Thereafter Vuhi, the Goat, and Dinas, the Ram, lived on in the forest untroubled by the Wolves.

"Here are three of us and see, here on the floor is our harvest already divided into three heaps"

ADVENTURE IX

THE HARVEST

Well, the time came when the field of barley which the Fox and the Wolf had planted together was ready to harvest. So the two friends cut the grain and carried the sheaves to the threshing barn where they spread them out to dry.

When it was time to thresh the grain, they asked Osmo, the Bear, to come and help them.

"Certainly," Osmo said.

At the time agreed the three animals met at the threshing barn.

"Now the first thing to decide," Pekka said, "is how to divide the work."

The Fox climbed nimbly up to the rafters.

"I'll stay up here," he called down, "and support the beams and the rafters. In that way there won't be any danger of their falling and injuring either of you. You two work down there without any concern. Trust me! I'll take care of you!"

So Osmo, the Bear, used the flail, and Pekka, the Wolf, winnowed the chaff from the grain. Mikko, the rascal, occasionally dropped down upon them a hunk of wood.

"Take care!" they'd call out. "Do you want to kill us?"

"Indeed, brothers, you have no idea how hard it is for me to hold up all these rafters!" Mikko would say. "You're very lucky it's only a little piece that drops on you now and then! If it weren't for me you'd certainly be killed, both of you!"

Well, the Bear and the Wolf worked steadily. When they were finished Mikko, the rascal, leaped down from the rafters and stretched himself as though he had been working the hardest of them all.

"I'm glad that job of mine is finished!" he said. "I couldn't have held things up much longer!"

"Well now," Pekka asked, "how shall we divide this our harvest?"

"I'll tell you how," Mikko said. "Here are three of us and, see, here on the floor is our harvest already divided into three heaps. The biggest heap will naturally go to the biggest of us. That's Osmo, the Bear. The middle sized heap will go to you, Pekka. I'm the smallest, so the smallest heap comes to me."

The Bear and the Wolf, stupid old things, agreed to this. So Osmo took the great heap of straw, Pekka the pile of chaff, and Mikko, the rascal, got for his share the little mound of clean grain.

Together they all went to the mill to grind their meal.

As the millstone turned on Mikko's grain, it made a rough rasping sound.

"Strange," Osmo said to Pekka, "Mikko's grain sounds different from ours."

"Mix some sand with yours," Mikko said, "then yours will make the same sound."

So the Bear and the Wolf poured some sand in their straw and their chaff and sure enough, when they turned their millstones again, they, too, got a rough rasping sound.

This satisfied them and they went home feeling they had just as good a winter's supply of food as Mikko.

He dropped it in the water and of course it spread out far and wide and the current carried it off

ADVENTURE X

THE PORRIDGE

Well, it was only natural that they should all want to see at once what kind of porridge their meal would make.

Osmo's came out black and disgusting. Greatly disturbed he ambled over to Mikko's house for advice. The Fox was stirring his own porridge which was white and smooth.

"What's the matter with my porridge?" the Bear asked. "Yours is white and smooth but mine is black and horrid."

"Did you wash your meal before you put it into the pot?" the Fox asked.

"Wash it? No! How do you wash meal?"

"You take it to the river and drop it in the water. Then when it's clean you take it out."

The Bear at once went home and got his ground up straw and took it to the river. He dropped it in the water and of course it spread out far and wide and the current carried it off.

So that was the end of Osmo's share of the harvest.

Pekka, the Wolf, had as little luck with his porridge. Soon he, too, came to Mikko for advice.

"I don't know what's the matter with me," he said. "I don't seem to be able to make good porridge. Look at yours all white and smooth! I must watch you how you make it. Won't you let me hang my pot on your crane? Then I'll do just as you do."

"Certainly," the Fox said. "Hang your pot on this chain and the two pots can then cook side by side."

"Yours is so white to begin with," Pekka said, "and mine looks no better than dirt."

"Before you came I climbed up the chain and hung over the pot," the Fox said. "The heat of the fire melted the fat in my tail and it dripped down into the pot. It's that fat that makes my porridge look so white."

Poor gullible Pekka immediately suspended himself on the chain above his porridge. But he didn't stay there long. The flames scorched him and he fell down hurting his side. If you notice, to this day any Wolf that you meet has stiff sides that make it hard for him to turn and twist, and to this day all Wolves smell of burnt hair.

Well, Pekka, after he had got his breath, tasted his porridge again to see if it was any better. But it wasn't. It was as bad as ever.

"I don't see any difference in it," he said. "Let me taste yours, Mikko."

The Fox artfully scooped up a spoonful of the Wolf's porridge and dropped it into his own pot.

"Help yourself," he said. "Take some out of that spot there. That's good."

The place he pointed to was, of course, the place where he had dropped some of the Wolf's own porridge.

So poor old stupid Pekka only sampled his own porridge again when he thought he was tasting Mikko's.

"Strange," he said, "your porridge doesn't taste good to me either. I don't believe anything tastes good to me to-day. The truth is I don't believe I like porridge."

He went home sad and discouraged while Mikko, the rascal, chuckled to himself and said:

"I wonder why Pekka doesn't like porridge. It tastes awful good to me!"

ADVENTURE XI

NURSE MIKKO

The Wolf's wife gave birth to three little cubs and then died.

"You poor children!" Pekka said, "your mother is dead and there is no one to take her place. I must get you a nurse."

So he went through the forest hunting some one to take care of his motherless cubs. The white Grouse offered her services but, when she sang a lullaby to show what a good nurse she could be, Pekka shook his head.

"I don't like your voice," he said. "I can't take you."

Then Jussi, the Hare, applied for the position.

"You know I'm lame," he said, "so quiet work like nursing would suit me."

"Can you sing lullabies?" Pekka asked.

"Oh, yes! Listen!" and Jussi began squealing.

"Stop!" Pekka cried. "I don't like your voice either."

Just then Mikko, the Fox, came running up.

"Good day, Pekka," he said. "I hear you're out looking for a nurse for your sweet babies."

"Yes, Mikko, I am. Can you recommend one?"

"I'd like the job myself," the Fox said.

"You, Mikko?"

"Yes."

"But you can't sing lullabies, can you?"

"Oh, yes! I sing them very beautifully. Listen:

'Hushabye, sweet little cubs,
 Hushabye to sleep!
Who best loves you, do you think?
Who will give you food and drink?
Who on faithful guard will keep?
 Mikko! Mikko!

'Hushabye, sweet little cubs,
 Mikko loves you well,
Loves each little pointed nose,
Loves your little scratchy toes,
Loves you more than he can tell—
 Mikko! Mikko!'"

He ran after Mikko and was about to overtake him when Mikko slipped into a crevice in the rocks. Only one paw stuck out

Pekka, the Wolf, was charmed with Mikko's lullaby.

"Beautiful! Beautiful!" he said. "I never heard a sweeter lullaby! You're the very nurse I want! Come home with me at once."

So Mikko went home with Pekka and took over the care of the three little Wolf cubs.

"I'll go off now and get them something to eat," Pekka said.

He came back after a while with the hind leg of a horse.

"This will be enough for them to start on," he said.

The Fox shook his head.

"I'm afraid it won't last them very long. They're beautiful healthy children with fine appetites."

"Poor little dears!" Pekka said. "Let me see them."

"Not just now!" Mikko insisted. "They're asleep and mustn't be disturbed. Go out hunting again and the next time you come home you shall see them."

Pekka felt that the Fox must be a very good nurse indeed to be so strict. So he went off hunting again without seeing his children.

As soon as he was gone Mikko, the rascal, ate up all the horse meat without giving the cubs one bite and then, as he was still hungry, he ate one of the cubs. The next day he ate another cub, and the day following he ate the last of them. He was just finishing that last cub when the Wolf came home and called in at the door:

"Now, nurse, here I am come home to see my dear children! They're well, aren't they?"

"Very well!" the Fox declared. "But they've grown so big under my good care that the house isn't large enough now to hold them and you and me at the same time. If you're coming in, I must get out first."

So the Wolf stood aside as the Fox came out and scampered away.

Then the Wolf went in and of course all he could find of his dear children were their bones.

"You faithless, faithless nurse!" he cried.

In awful rage he ran after Mikko and was about to overtake him when Mikko slipped into a crevice in the rocks. Only one paw stuck out. The Wolf pounced on this paw and began gnawing it.

"Say, Pekka, have you gone crazy?" the Fox asked. "What do you think you're doing biting that old root? I hope you don't think it's one of my paws. I'm sitting on all four paws."

The Wolf looked up to see whether this was true and, quick as a flash, Mikko, the rascal, drew in his paw.

So the poor old Wolf, fooled again, went sadly home.

Of course the instant he opened his mouth the Grouse flew away

ADVENTURE XII

THE BEAR SAYS *NORTH*

 One day while Osmo, the Bear, was prowling about the woods he caught a Grouse.

"Pretty good!" he thought to himself. "Wouldn't the other animals be surprised if they knew old Osmo had caught a Grouse!"

He was so proud of his feat that he wanted all the world to know of it. So, holding the Grouse carefully in his teeth without injuring it, he began parading up and down the forest ways.

"They'll all certainly envy me this nice plump Grouse," he thought. "And they won't be so ready to call me awkward and lumbering after this, either!"

Presently Mikko, the Fox, sauntered by. He saw at once that Osmo was showing off and he determined that the Bear would not get the satisfacion of any admiration from him. So he pretended not to see the Grouse at all. Instead he pointed his nose upwards and sniffed.

"Um! Um!" grunted Osmo, trying to attract attention to himself.

"Ah," Mikko remarked, casually, "is that you, Osmo? What way is the wind blowing to-day? Can you tell me?"

Osmo, of course, could not answer without opening his mouth, so he grunted again hoping that Mikko would have to notice why he couldn't answer. But the Fox didn't glance at him at all. With his nose still pointed upwards he kept sniffing the air.

"It seems to me it's from the South," he said. "Isn't it from the South, Osmo?"

"Um! Um! Um!" the Bear grunted.

"You say it is from the South, Osmo? Are you sure?"

"Um! Um!" Osmo repeated, growing every moment more impatient.

"Oh, not from the South, you say. Then from what direction is it blowing?"

THE BEAR SAYS *NORTH*

By this time the Bear was so exasperated by Mikko's interest in the wind when he should have been admiring the Grouse that he forgot himself, opened his mouth, and roared out:

"North!"

Of course the instant he opened his mouth, the Grouse flew away.

"Now see what you've done!" he stormed angrily. "You've made me lose my fine plump Grouse!"

"I?" Mikko asked. "What had I to do with it?"

"You kept asking me about the wind until I opened my mouth—that's what you did!"

The Fox shrugged his shoulders.

"Why did you open your mouth?"

"Well, you can't say, 'North!' without opening your mouth, can you?" the Bear demanded.

The Fox laughed heartily.

"See here, Osmo, don't blame me. Blame yourself. If I had had that Grouse in my mouth and you had asked me about the wind, I should never have said, 'North!'"

"What would you have said?" the Bear asked.

Mikko, the rascal, laughed harder than ever. Then he clenched his teeth and said:

"East!"

"Why, do you know," he said,
"my turnips and my bread
don't taste a bit like this!"

ADVENTURE XIII

OSMO'S SHARE

One day Osmo, the Bear, came to a clearing where a Man was plowing.

"Good day," the Bear said. "What are you doing?"

"I'm plowing," the Man answered. "After I finish plowing I'm going to harrow and then plant the field, half in wheat and half in turnips."

"Yum! Yum!" Osmo thought to himself. "Good food that—wheat and turnips!"

Aloud he said:

"I know how to plow and harrow. What do you say to my helping you?"

"If you help me," the Man said, "I'll share the harvest with you."

So Osmo set to work and between them they soon had the field plowed, harrowed, and planted.

When Autumn came they went to get their crops.

At the turnip field the Man said:

"Now what do you want as your share—the part that grows above the ground or the part that grows below?"

Osmo, the Bear, seeing how green and luxuriant the turnip tops were, said:

"Give me the part that grows above ground."

After they had harvested the turnips, they went on to the wheat field where the Man put the same question.

The wheat stocks were all dry and shriveled. Osmo looked at them wisely and said:

"This time you better give me the part that grows under the ground."

The Man laughed in his sleeve and agreed.

One day the following winter the two met and the Man invited the Bear to dinner. Osmo who was very hungry accepted the invitation gladly.

First they had baked turnips.

"Oh, but these are good!" Osmo said. "I've never tasted anything better! What are they!"

"Why," the Man said, "they're the turnips from that field that you and I planted together."

The Bear was greatly surprised.

Then they had some freshly baked bread.

"How good! How good!" Osmo exclaimed. "What is it?"

"Just plain bread," the Man said, "baked from the wheat you and I planted together."

Osmo was more surprised than ever.

"Why, do you know," he said, "my turnips and my bread don't taste a bit like this!"

The Man burst out laughing and Osmo wondered why.

The first person they met was an old Horse. They put their case to him

ADVENTURE XIV

THE REWARD OF KINDNESS

 Osmo, the Bear, used to go day after day to a field of growing rye and eat as much as he wanted. The Farmer noticed from the Bear's tracks that he always came by the same route.

"I'll teach that Bear a lesson!" the Farmer thought to himself.

So he set a snare made of a strong net and carefully covered it over with leaves and branches.

That day Osmo, when he came as usual to the field, got entangled in the net and was unable to escape.

The Farmer when he came and found him securely caught was overjoyed.

"Now, you brute!" he said, 'I've got you and I'm going to kill you!"

"Oh, master, don't do that!" the Bear implored. "Don't kill me!"

"Why shouldn't I kill you?" the Farmer asked. "Aren't you destroying my rye?"

"Let me off this time!" Osmo begged, "and I'll reward you! I swear I will!"

He begged and begged until at last he prevailed upon the Farmer to open the net and let him out.

"Now then," the Farmer said as soon as the Bear was freed, "how are you going to reward me?"

Osmo put a heavy paw on the Farmer's shoulder.

"This is how I'm going to reward you," he said: "I'm going to eat you up!"

"What!" the Farmer exclaimed, "is that your idea of a reward for kindness?"

"Exactly!" Osmo declared. "In this world that is the reward kindness always gets! Ask any one!"

"I don't believe it! I don't believe it!" the Farmer cried.

"Very well. I'll prove to you that I'm right. We'll ask the first person we meet."

The first person they met was an old Horse. They put their case to him.

"The Bear is right," the old Horse said. "Look at me: For thirty years I gave my master faithful service and just this morning I heard him say: 'It's time we killed that old plug! He's no good for work any more and he's only eating his head off!'"

The Bear squinted his little eyes.

"You see!"

"No, I don't see!" the Farmer insisted. "We must ask some one else."

They walked on a little farther until they met an old Dog. They put their case to him and at once the Dog said:

"The Bear is right! Look at me: I gave my master a life time of faithful service and just this morning I overheard him say: 'It's time we killed that old Dog!' Alas, alas, in this wicked world goodness is always so rewarded!"

But still the Farmer was unsatisfied and to humor him Osmo said that he was willing that they should put their case once more to the judgment of an outsider.

The next person they met was Mikko, the Fox. Mikko listened carefully and then drawing the Farmer aside he whispered:

"If I give judgment in your favor will you let me carry off all the chickens in your hen-house?"

"Indeed I will!" the Farmer promised.

Then Mikko cleared his throat importantly and said:

"H'm! H'm! To give fair judgment in this case I must go over all the ground. First show me the field of rye and the damage Osmo did."

So they went to the field and the Fox, after he had appraised the damage, shook his head seriously.

"It was certainly wicked of Osmo eating all that rye! . . . Now show me the net."

So they went to the snare and the Fox examined it carefully.

"You say the Bear got entangled in this snare. I want to see just how he did it."

Osmo showed just how he had been caught.

"Get all the way in," the Fox said. "I want to make sure that you couldn't possibly get out unaided."

So the Bear entangled himself again in the net and proved that he couldn't possibly get out unaided.

"Well," said Mikko, the rascal, "you deserved to get caught the first time and now that you're in there again you can just stay there! Come on, Mr. Farmer."

So Mikko and the Farmer went off leaving Osmo to his fate.

That night the Fox went to the Farmer's hen-house to claim his reward. When he came in the chickens, of course, set up an awful squawking that aroused the family. The Farmer stayed in bed but he sent his wife out with a stout club.

"It sounds to me," he said, "as if some rascally Fox is trying to steal our hens. If you catch him, don't be gentle with him!"

"Gentle!" repeated the wife significantly.

She hurried out to the hen-house and when she found Mikko inside she gave him an awful beating. In fact he barely escaped with his life.

"Ah!" he said to himself as he limped painfully home, "to think that this is the reward my kindness has received! Oh, what a wicked, wicked world this is!"

With that the Bear lifted his paw and the little mouse scampered off

ADVENTURE XV

THE BEAR AND THE MOUSE

When Osmo, the Bear, was left alone in the net, he thrashed about this way and that until he was exhausted. Then he fell asleep.

While he slept a host of little Mice began playing all over his great body. Their tiny feet tickled him and he woke with a start. The Mice scampered off, all but one that Osmo caught under his paw.

"Tweek! Tweek!" the frightened little Mouse cried. "Let me go! Let me go! Please let me go! If you do I'll reward you some day! I promise I will!"

Osmo let out a great roar of laughter.

"What, little one? You'll reward me! Ha! Ha! That is good! The Mouse will reward the Bear! Well now, that is a joke! However, little one, I will let you go! You're too weak and insignificant for me to kill and too small to eat. So run along!"

With that the Bear lifted his paw and the little Mouse scampered off.

"It will reward me for my kindness!" Osmo repeated, and in spite of the fact that he was fast caught in a net he shook again with laughter.

He was still laughing when the little Mouse returned with a great army of his fellows. All the host at once began gnawing at the ropes of the net and in no time at all they had freed the big Bear.

"You see," the little Mouse said, "although we are weak and insignificant we can reward a kindness!"

Osmo was so ashamed for having laughed at the Mice on account of their size that all he could say as he shambled off into the forest was:

"Thanks!"

ADVENTURE XVI

THE LAST OF OSMO

There was a Farmer that used to drive his sledge into the forest to cut wood. Always as he drove he shouted abusively at his Horse.

"Go along, you old plug!" he'd say.

"What do you think you're good for, anyway? If you don't move along more lively I'll give you to the Bear for his supper—that's what I'll do with you!"

Now Osmo, the Bear, heard about this, how the Farmer was always talking about giving him his Horse, so one afternoon while the Farmer was going through his usual tirade Osmo suddenly stepped out of the bushes and said:

"Well, Mr. Farmer, here I am! Suppose you give me my supper."

The Farmer was greatly taken back.

"I didn't really mean what I was saying," he stammered. "He's a good Horse but he's a little lazy—that's all."

Osmo stood there swaying his shoulders and twisting his head.

"Even if he is lazy he'll taste all right to me. Come along, Mr. Farmer, hand him over as you've promised to do this long time!"

"But I can't afford to give you my Horse!" the Farmer cried. "He's the only Horse I've got!"

But the Bear was firm.

"No matter! You have to keep your word!"

"See here," the Farmer begged, "let me off on giving you my Horse and I tell you what I'll do: I'll give you my Cow. I can spare the Cow better."

"When will you give me the Cow?" the Bear asked.

"To-morrow," the Farmer promised.

"Very well," Osmo said, "if you deliver me the Cow to-morrow I'll let you off on the Horse. But see you keep your word!"

On his way home that afternoon the Farmer visited his traps. In one he found Mikko, the Fox. Mikko, the little rascal, begged for his life so piteously that the Farmer with a laugh freed him.

"You've done me a good turn," Mikko said, "and some day I'll do something for you. Just wait and see if I don't."

Well, early next morning the Farmer put his Cow on the sledge and started off for the forest. On the way he met Mikko.

"Good morning," Mikko said. "Where are you going with your Cow?"

The Farmer stopped and told Mikko about his bargain with the Bear.

"See here," the Fox said, "I promised you yesterday that some day I'd do you a good turn. That day has come! I'm going to save you your Cow and show you how you can kill that old Bear once and for all. But if I do this, you'll have to give me the Bear's carcass after he's dead and gone."

"I'll be glad enough to do that," the Farmer declared. "Save me my Cow and you may have all of that old Bear that you want!"

"Well then," Mikko said, "go home with the Cow as quickly as you can and come back here with ten distaffs.

My plan is to have you put five of the distaffs around my neck and five around my tail. I can make an awful noise rattling them. When the Bear hears me and wonders who I am, do you say to him: 'Oh! That must be my son, the Hunter! Don't you hear the rattle of his musket?' Then between us we'll finish that old Bear."

The Farmer did as the Fox directed. He drove the Cow home and returned to the forest with ten distaffs, five of which he fastened about the Fox's neck and five about his tail. Then he drove the sledge on to the place where he was to meet the Bear and Mikko, the Fox, crept along quietly behind him.

"Where's my Cow?" the Bear demanded as soon as the sledge appeared.

"I've come to talk to you about that," the Farmer began.

Just then there was an awful rattle of something in the bushes behind the Farmer.

"What's that?" the Bear cried.

"Oh," the Farmer said, "that must be my son, the Hunter! Don't you hear the rattle of his musket?"

The Bear shook in terror.

"The Hunter, you say! Mercy me, what shall I do! Oh, Mr. Farmer, save me from the Hunter and I'll forgive you the Cow!"

"Very well," the Farmer promised, "I'll do my best! Lie down and I'll try to make the Hunter believe you're only a log."

So the Bear lay down on the ground and stayed perfectly quiet.

"Father," called the Fox in a voice that sounded like the Hunter's, "what's that big brown thing lying on the ground near you? Is it a Bear?"

"No, son," the Farmer called back, "that isn't a Bear. It's only a log of wood."

"If it's a log of wood, father, chop it up!"

The Farmer raised his ax.

"Don't really chop me!" the Bear begged in a whisper. "Just pretend to."

"This is too good a log to chop up," the Farmer said.

"Well, father," said the voice from the bushes, "if it's such a good log you better put it on your sledge and take it home."

"Lie still," the Farmer whispered, "while I put you on the sledge."

So the Bear lay stiff and quiet and the Farmer dragged him on to the sledge.

"Father," the voice said, "you better tie that log down to keep it from rolling off."

"Don't move," the Farmer whispered, "and I'll tie you down just as if you were a log."

So the Bear lay perfectly still while the Farmer lashed him securely to the sledge.

"Father, are you sure that log can't roll off?"

"Yes, son," the Farmer said, "I'm sure it can't roll off now."

"Then, father, drive your ax into the end of the log and off we'll go!"

At that the Farmer raised his ax and with one mighty blow buried it in the neck of the Bear.

So that was the end of poor old lumbering Osmo!

The Farmer was saved both his Horse and his Cow and Mikko, the rascal, feasted on Bear meat for a week.

So that was THE END

Lightning Source UK Ltd.
Milton Keynes UK
UKHW02f0629191217
314746UK00005B/502/P